R. HUDSON POPE

R. HUDSON POPE

R. HUDSON POPE

A BIOGRAPHY BY
PATRICIA M. ST. JOHN

with an Introduction
by John M. Laird

SCRIPTURE UNION
5 WIGMORE STREET, LONDON, W.1

© Patricia M. St. John 1967
First published 1967

Printed in Great Britain
by Billing & Sons Limited, Guildford and London

BV
3785
.P6
S2

Contents

CHAPTER		PAGE
	Introduction by John M. Laird, General Secretary Scripture Union 1946–67	7
1	"Prayer-destined by Mother and Father"	16
2	"Dick, You Must Do Something"	23
3	Comedian and Editor	32
4	"I Didn't Shine all the Time"	38
5	On Trial with the C.S.S.M.	47
6	Ethel Stacey and her Spartans	56
7	Secrets of Success	65
8	Did the Converts Last?	72
9	Sand and Sunshine by the Sea	79
10	He Taught Others to Expect Conversions	87
11	The Friend of Hundreds of Boys	93
12	"Another Member Sends 4d."	101
13	Never Under-rate the Under-eights	106
14	God's Gentleness Made Him Great	112
15	The Joy of Arrival	116

Introduction

BY JOHN M. LAIRD,
GENERAL SECRETARY, SCRIPTURE UNION 1946–67

THE name of Richard Hudson Pope has been a legend in our family for as long as I can remember. One of my aunts was in his seaside mission house-party at Seamill, in Scotland, for instance, where the mission team included the late Archibald Fleming, first Bishop to the Arctic. When I was on the mission team at Elie, and R. H. P. was leading the mission at St. Andrews, we saw a little of each other, and I remember the look on his face, and the joy he showed, when he heard of some encouraging meetings that we had had.

It must have been about 1926 that R. H. P. gave some Bible readings on the second coming of Christ at one of the first Scottish I.V.F. conferences held at St. Andrews. I still treasure the notes I took then. Although R. H. P. had had no formal theological or Bible College training, these lectures were the best, the clearest, the sanest, and the most satisfying that I have heard on that particular subject.

In 1939, the year of the Diamond Jubilee of the Scripture Union method of Bible reading, we were travelling round speaking at meetings together. I had a film which I was showing. At a number of places we had difficulty with blackout arrangements, and spent many busy hours making ingenious arrangements to darken the windows of church halls, for it was light in the evenings. On one occasion, however, it looked as if we were beaten, for the meeting was to be in the Town Hall of a large northern city, well known to R. H. P. He warned me that there were large clear-glass windows all round it, which could not possibly be blacked-out. On the way, we pulled up by the roadside and prayed about it. It turned out to be a dull, rather foggy evening. We left the film to the end of the meeting. When we showed it, the hall was surprisingly dark, and the pictures showed up well. Next day we read that there had been a partial eclipse of the sun, and this had combined with the dull evening to give us all the 'blackout' we needed! Needless to say, neither of us felt that a partial eclipse of the sun had been specially arranged to suit our convenience, but we took what came with thankfulness, nevertheless.

R. H. P. was no ascetic, and he enjoyed a good meal: "preaching is hungry work", he would say with a twinkle.

It is no doubt true that, as Miss St. John suggests, he did not spend long times in prayer—at least, not as compared with other great saints of the Christian Church. But I remember occupying a room next to his at the High Leigh Conference centre, and hearing his voice very quietly in the early morning. I could not hear the words, but it seemed as if he was going through a prayer-list, mentioning aloud a series of names and pausing for a few moments after each one. He had a large, very well-worn Bible, in the back of which were many small photographs of boys for whom he prayed, probably very regularly.

Richard Hudson Pope was a man of vision and of singleness of purpose. He had a deeply devout Christian mother. Like many of the great saints of the Church, he was a practical mystic, with an emphasis on the practical. Above all, Christ was a reality to him; he made Christ real to others, and, in the end, he surely became one of the most Christlike men that any of us have known. It has been said that the single common ingredient of all greatness is the quality of persistence—an infinite capacity for taking pains. This quality R. H. P. possessed in marked degree, and all his persistence was directed towards knowing Christ and making Him known. For him it was: "One thing I know . . . one thing I do."

He was, of course, as we all are, a child of his age—his character was largely formed fifty years before the publication of this book. And, in the course of that half-century, revolutionary changes—perhaps unparalleled in range and speed in any half-century in history—have taken place.

It is not surprising, therefore, if for many younger readers R. H. P. seems to belong to, and speak in the idiom of, another age. As we read of his childhood home and early youth, we are taken right back into the atmosphere of a deeply pious late Victorian home. By 1914, one of the great watersheds of human history, and the beginning of the end of an outstanding period of Christian faith and vitality, R. H. P. had already served for eight years as a children's evangelist. But he carried through into the inter-war period, and even beyond 1945, the message and the emphases of his early training, and these were still immensely effective. Now, in 1967, his preaching is over, his work is done. As we look back, we can see that he was one of the wisest, most skilful, and most effective and widely used children's evangelists of 'modern' times.

He was God's messenger for that particular generation. For God has His prophets in every generation, each with his own distinctive message, each different from the other, each presenting His message in a different way, each with his own special emphasis. Prophets, of all people, are not mass-produced. Each mould in which a prophet is fashioned is broken, never to be used again. Some have been scholars and statesmen—Moses, Isaiah, Paul, Augustine, Calvin, Wesley. Others had little formal education—Amos, Francis of Assisi, George Fox, D. L. Moody—and Richard Hudson Pope.

It was because R. H. P. was a child of his age that he was able to speak to the children of his own age in their own idiom. As R. H. P. said of himself, "One of me is enough! If it hadn't been so, God would have made more. (His aim is) not to repeat me, but to make a well-trained, well-disciplined *you* for His glory. It is thus that veterans in God's service are made. There is no short cut to a blessed ministry. It was blood and tears and sweat for Him to make it possible for us, and it will mean blood and sweat for you and me to come to the realization, and to reach the Lord."

Yet, wherever there is an authentic prophet of God, there is a timeless quality about his personality and his message, and it is this that we look for and find as we read the story of R. H. P.

The children's evangelist or Sunday school teacher of today must endeavour to mediate the Gospel through his own words and personality. There is a rightful sense in which, in all humility, he must not be afraid to be himself, and to place the emphasis where God would have him place it. Yet that same personality must be subjected to the long training process which is God's purpose for each of us. When R. H. P. was young he was a "naturally gifted, self-opinionated young man, with a certain amount of self-confidence". This book shows how God's moulding hand was upon him through experience and personal sorrow, and how gradually he perfected his craft, over many years, by unremitting work. "You cannot slide into spiritual experience," he said, "you must climb to it." There were no short cuts to sanctification; there was no 'easy believism' for him. The battle had to be fought, as John Bunyan so vividly taught, all the way from the City of Destruction, right up to the very gates of the Celestial City itself.

Not only is there a difference between the men of one age and another, but there are also great differences between one man and another of the same generation. Very different from R. H. P. were his contemporaries within our own movement. R. T. Archibald was the personal worker, the speaker to small groups, the master of the magic lantern, the indefatigable writer of letters ("we need epistleship as well as apostleship"), the most perfect of Christian gentlemen in the best sense of the word and the disciplined Christian soldier. There was Edmund Clark, the genius, with some of the faults of a genius, the man whose legendary skill in driving home a point by acting out a situation on the spur of the moment, is proverbial among us. One year, at Sheringham, at a boys' camp, a distinguished visitor was about to leave for Norwich. There were two seats available in the car, and Edmund Clark was asked to find two boys who would like the drive into town. In those days, a lift in a car was quite a special privilege; the question was how to select the privileged two. So Mr. Clark strolled across the field where boys were playing informally around. He picked up a couple of empty buckets and made his way to the tap to collect water for the cookhouse. Slowly he sauntered across the field with the empty buckets. Presently up came two boys—"Mr. Clark, can we get the water for you?" "Thank you, no need ... but would you like a lift into Norwich? There are two seats available if you hurry!" This is but one of hundreds of examples in teaching practical Christianity.

Very different again were the dignified Goodman brothers. George, the past master in clarity and simplicity in teaching doctrine, and in expressing it in pellucid English, both in spoken and written form; Montague, the vivid, sometimes dramatic, Bible storyteller, the systematic teacher with the unforgettable illustrations, the writer of best-sellers for boys, and the compelling speaker, with the mannerisms which boys delighted to imitate. There was Frank Millard, the epitome of muscular Christianity, the perfectionist in running a camp and building a sand pulpit, the winner of boys and the trainer of Christian workers, more by example than by words, and whose work in South Africa has so splendidly stood the test of time. And Bishop Taylor Smith, the burly and beloved President of the C.S.S.M. for so many years, the maker of parables and nuggetty phrases that stuck in the mind for a lifetime.

Each one was different from the other. Yet they have left us a certain apostolic succession, a tradition, which is one of our greatest possessions as a movement.

One is tempted to say that these were the great men, and that we shall not see their like again. But these men are gone, though the record of them remains for our instruction. Our need today is not for imitators, but for contemporary prophets, to give to us and to our children the Word from the Lord which we so greatly need. We need not doubt for a moment that God is still sending us such men, but we need to support them with our love and prayers, for without that their courage may fail and their word may be in vain.

R. H. P. was always thinking about other people, yet never in a self-assertive way; he was energetic, but not aggressively so; he was cheerful, and humorous, but his humour was never laboured, second-rate or at the expense of others; he possessed a native courtesy—a little old-fashioned, of course, but all the more charming for that. He had charm, but it was the charm of inner goodness shining through his personality.

He was a man of deep integrity of character, and his whole life and witness were consistent right through. His keen moral sense of right and wrong was expressed in practical ways, and yet tempered, especially in later years, with kindly sympathy and understanding for his weaker brother. His innate honesty meant that he did not exaggerate or claim too much in speaking about his work.

Along with this went his care for the individual, especially as seen in his faithful letter-writing in following up his Scripture Union branch members, and in his holding on for them in prayer, often for years.

He enjoyed the inestimable gift of excellent health, and this he dedicated unreservedly to his Master's service, working with abounding energy. But it was not mere activism, for all he did seemed to be irradiated with faith, hope, and love.

The solid childhood foundation of doctrine and principle formed a basis on which he built up an ever-increasing store of applied common sense and practical wisdom. It was this which saved him from adopting unbalanced doctrines of sanctification. He had no need for them, nor had we who knew him. His life and example were the best answer. Those trained by him needed no other contemporary text-book to show what it meant to live a holy life.

He was absolutely loyal to the Council and the Society which he served. He never spoke disparagingly of those who were over him. When decisions were made or policies followed which he disagreed with, one could sometimes sense that he might feel disappointed or sad, but that was all. There was never, so far as I know, anything which marred his relationships with the Council of the movement or the General Secretary. When a new General Secretary, a man much younger than himself, was appointed in 1946, he wrote at once to pay his 'respects to the Secretarial Chair' and to pledge his loyalty. His monthly reports and expenses sheets were punctiliously dealt with in his clear handwriting.

Perhaps the main criticism that has been made of R. H. P. has been about his emphasis on sin in his preaching to children. More than one critic felt that he was in danger of inducing a sense of guilt in the minds of sensitive, conscientious children which could be harmful. It is possible that there may have been some element of truth in this criticism in a few cases.

But when you listened to what he actually said, and the way in which he said it, there seemed to be a complete freedom from any trace of morbidity. The seriousness, and even at times the solemnity, of his message was lightened by touches of warm humanity and wit. It was not so much that he emphasized sin, but that there was such a sense of the greatness and holiness and majesty of God present in the meeting that we felt like Peter—"Depart from me, for I am a sinful man, O Lord". The illustrations he gave of what he meant by sin were always practical and down-to-earth—selfishness and thoughtlessness for others being illustrated by being unkind to Grandmother, or slamming doors. Cheating, telling lies, dishonesty, were illustrated by homely incidents about a young man in his first office job.

There were references to impurity and bad habits in his public meetings, and explicit talks on sex in special meetings for boys. There was no doubt an Edwardian flavour about these, but his tremendous sense of the fitness of things, his wholesomeness, honesty and sense of humour, his practical good sense and his long experience in counselling, combined to make him a wise guide.

Above all, he was always quick to apply the remedy. It is safe to say that there was never a reference to sin that was not closely coupled with a clear presentation of the solution to the problem, and the healing of the wound; if there was sorrow, he was quick to comfort; if there was a sense of guilt, he was quick to point out the promises of forgiveness; if there was perplexity, there would be a carefully thought out and sensible attempt to explain.

In his retirement speech, R. H. P. emphasized that we are the Children's Special Service Mission, and must remain so. He was referring, no doubt, to the value of evangelistic missions to children. In attempting to assess the validity of this plea in modern conditions, we have to remember, first, that R. H. P. always regarded his evangelism as building on a groundwork of Christian teaching. He referred to the evangelist as the 'special agent' who must not relieve the parents of 'their duty to God in bringing up their children in the fear of the Lord, instructing them in the Scriptures, and endeavouring to lead them to the Saviour'. In addition, 'his plan was to work with the Sunday schools and churches, and he left the preparation of his missions to the teachers'; his own task was to 'kindle the fuel that had probably been patiently laid for years, to lead the well-instructed children to Christ, and then to hand them back to their own teachers for subsequent building-up and Christian fellowship'.

His old friend Mr. Edward Olney said of him that he never planted a tree until he had made sure that a good hole had been dug for it. On this principle there will always remain the need for children's evangelism.

There are, however, those who claim that evangelistic missions should be arranged for children even where there has been little preparatory teaching and as little provision for follow-up. They suggest that, if children's missions are not held in the really needy or pagan areas, then such children may never have an opportunity to hear the Gospel. But the answer surely is that what such children need is in the first instance not an evangelistic mission, but a Sunday school or its equivalent, so that a good foundation of teaching can prepare the way in due course for the reaper-evangelist.

It is also argued that God can surely, in His sovereignty, cause a child to be converted through hearing the Gospel preached even though that child has had no preparatory teaching. Of course this is true, and certainly this can and does happen. But no settled policy of evangelism should be based on what would appear to be God's exceptional ways of working.

If it is true, as it may well be, that there are today far fewer Christian homes and far fewer churches and Sunday schools where children are well taught and carefully prepared in Christian doctrine and Bible knowledge, then we must conclude that the scope for evangelism in the specialized sense must be more limited and the emphasis adjusted. But in evangelism, as in much else, what may be lacking in quantity can be compensated for in quality and depth, and often the most lasting and far-reaching effects flow from concentration on a small group. If, therefore, it is suggested that in this post-Christian and, in some areas, largely pagan age, we should endeavour to build up an ever-increasing team of children's evangelists at the expense of a regular teaching ministry, the writer submits that this would not appear to be God's special commission to us today. That this concentration of staff on evangelism was God's commission to our fathers in the faith earlier in our Society's history we do not doubt for a moment. But with the rise of the camping movement following the First World War, and the Inter-School Fellowship after 1945, together with a whole range of new developments in recent years, we can surely discern the Holy Spirit's leading into new and, for our day, very effective and appropriate methods of presenting the Word of the Lord. These new developments include an ever-growing literature programme, a flourishing Sunday school department, and development in the whole field of evangelical witness in the educational world, all undergirded with a vigorous Bible-reading programme.

It is significant therefore that in 1960 the Council decided to change the registered name of our Society from Children's Special Service Mission to Scripture Union, though the initials 'C.S.S.M.' are still used for some of our evangelistic activities among children, and evangelism in the fullest sense remains one of the main aims of our movement. At the time of writing there are seventeen children's evangelists on the staff, and they are today becoming increasingly church-related, on the principle so wisely followed by R. H. P.

Introduction

Richard Hudson Pope, when he meets the One Whom he made so real to thousands of children, will leave behind him a living memorial. That memorial is a great company of men and women whom R. H. P. led to Christ when they were children and who are continuing faithfully in adult life and service. For it has often been noted that the converts of R. H. P.'s missions were marked by their staying qualities. Why was this? Partly because his was faithful and lucid teaching-evangelism; partly because he followed the principles we have just described; but, most of all, because in and through it all was the sovereign working of the Holy Spirit through a dedicated, consecrated man of God.

CHAPTER ONE

"Prayer-destined by Mother and Father"

In the summer of 1961 an old man in white flannels and a panama hat was rowed across the bay at Ballyholme in Northern Ireland, his boat being pulled ashore by a group of excited children.

A photograph of the incident appeared in *The Christian,* with a caption to remind the readers that the old man in the boat was the veteran children's evangelist, Richard Hudson Pope.

* * * * *

More than eighty years earlier, a Victorian mother, awaiting the birth of her seventh child, was reading an issue of that same periodical, *The Christian.* She was in a melancholy mood, for her father, John Cox, had recently died. He had been a loved pastor and preacher in Ipswich, and had founded the Burlington Chapel, and she grieved for him deeply. If only he had lived to give his blessing to the new baby! Somehow, the life that had passed and the life about to be given became inexorably linked in her mind. "Oh, Heavenly Father," she prayed, "if my baby is a boy, let him follow in his grandfather's footsteps. Let him be a preacher of the Gospel."

To her it was no chance, but a seal on her prayer, that the issue of *The Christian* that she was reading had in it a poem. She copied this poem out and the copy she made is still extant, written in beautiful, faded handwriting. The third verse ran as follows:

> And may thy voice His praises sing,
> And preach the Gospel of the King,
> And many a soul to Jesus bring,
>   Telling what He has done.
> Yet mayest thou ever humble be
> If great on earth, from pride set free,
> The Spirit always keeping thee
>   A happy little one.

Years later she wrote opposite it the glad words "being fulfilled". For the baby who was born on February 6th, 1879, was a boy who grew up to be a man of God and to spend his life leading boys and girls to Jesus Christ. And more than eighty years later, near the end of his lifetime of service, he was rowed across the bay at Ballyholme.

★ ★ ★ ★ ★

"Predestined by God to be conformed to the image of His Son," he wrote as an old man, "and prayer-destined by mother and father to be God's servant, I was brought up in a home where the love of God shone brightly through the love of godly parents, for whose influence and that of my brothers and sisters I can never be thankful enough."

Into this atmosphere of gentle love and prayer he was born, and he grew into a happy beloved little boy who wrote pious little hymns and rather gruesome ditties indiscriminately. As far as one can tell, he was not a remarkable child, but it must have been a remarkable home. So clearly and faithfully was the Bible taught, that eighty years later he was able to say, "I've often failed, but I've never doubted. I had all the answers before the doubts arrived." When people asked him, during the years of his ministry, how he had acquired his amazing knowledge of the Bible, his answer was always the same: "Mostly from my parents; I did not often have time to go to meetings and conventions later on." The greater part of those great doctrinal truths that he made so plain to children were learned from that gracious mother, or from Nell, the earnest, older sister of nineteen, who believed that piety begins at home, and seeing in her nine-year-old brother a lamb to be fed, held carefully prepared weekly Bible classes for him.

It is refreshing, in this age of rush and week-end travel, to look back to those peaceful nurseries of the middle-class Christian home of the last century. The days were uneventful on the whole, but in the Pope household at least, Sunday was a day of delight—a day when mother belonged entirely to her children, from the moment she buttoned them into their white sailor suits and frilly dresses, to the moment when she kissed them and blessed them and blew out the candle. From a very early age, all went to church with their parents, clutching pennies and little notebooks and pencils in which they took notes of the sermon—they were liable to be

B

cross-questioned at dinner-time on what they had heard! But the memory of Sunday mornings is not wearisome—rather it is a mingling of the sound of sweet church bells floating out over the town, of nestling up against mother—for it was always the privilege of the youngest to sit next to her—and going fast asleep—of happy anticipation of the delights to follow.

For Sunday afternoon was the highlight of the week. The same tireless mother gathered her seven round her and read them the simple, well-loved children's books of the day, *Line upon Line, Peep of Day, Children of India,* or *Children of China,* and, at a very early age, Dick purposed to become a foreign missionary. Once, when asked his name, the small boy looked up with due solemnity and replied, "Diddy Pope—missionawy to the Chinese".

There were delicious biscuits, too, in the shape of letters, which could be made into jumbled texts and gobbled up triumphantly when the puzzle was solved. There was a box of bricks which came out only on Sundays; there were texts to be coloured and subsequently given away to children in the street; and after a special Sunday tea there was a grand hymn-singing when the younger members of the family marched round the table to the strains of 'Onward, Christian soldiers', or sat on the carpet and 'pulled for the shore', or clustered round mother at the piano, leaning against her shoulder as they joined in the well-loved Gospel hymns. Then the little ones were bundled unwillingly to bed, and the older ones played Bible games, or just talked to mother.

Wonderful, golden days, with never a dull moment, but he understood later what they must have cost his parents in time and thought and preparation. They were well rewarded, for each of those children started life with a lasting impression that religion was warm and loving and attractive and joyful. Mother's gentle, secure presence drew them irresistibly round the Book—it was only a short step from there to the Saviour.

"I owe everything," he wrote, "firstly to God and His unspeakable riches of grace shown to us as children, and secondly to godly parents who were willing and able to be spent in showing us the joyfulness, the solemnity, the wonder, of God, His Word, and His day, in the light shining from the Lord Jesus Himself. Sometimes we played church; I don't remember any of the sermons we preached, but I do remember holding a communion service with my little sister. There was a bedroom water bottle, and a glass and a piece of bread, and we were in deadly earnest. Who shall say that the Lord was not present at His Table as Host to two little children who met to remember Him?"

The strict keeping of Sunday, and the value of home-training, were indelibly branded on him for life. Never could that day be passed over carelessly or lightly, and he, who served children so faithfully from the pulpit, always maintained that this was no substitute for the teaching of the Bible in the home.

"When an outside agent does anything for children", he wrote, "there is always the danger that the parents shall be relieved of their responsibility . . . nothing can relieve parents of their duty to God in bringing up their children in the fear of the Lord, instructing them in the Scriptures and endeavouring to lead them to the Saviour. Outside agencies should be auxiliary to the work of the parents and home, emphasizing in different words and through other lips the same truths which have been taught under the parental roof; thus the nail which has been driven into the board by the parents will be clinched on the other side by the outside agency."

And there were outside agencies in Dick's life. At nine years old he was sent for a time to a boarding school run by his Aunts Martha and Ruth. It was a good school, in every sense of the word, and Aunt Martha's discipline was lightened by Aunt Ruth's curls. Aunt Martha had no curls; she wore her hair piled on top of her head in the shape of a bread-basket. He never forgot the rivers on the east of England, or the sound Biblical teaching that he received at the school. Here, too, he was encouraged to go on with his music for which he had a real gift. He started learning the violin at the age of six, and he played the piano by ear, picking out tunes and harmonizing from memory from a very early age.

There was a memorable summer holiday too, when the family went to Pevensey, where Mr. Arrowsmith was conducting a C.S.S.M. Dick attended a boys' squash, and when decisions were asked for, he put up his hand. It seems to have been an emotional response that did not result in any decision at the time, but it was an emotion that persisted. He learned that night that there was some unmet need in his nine-year-old life. The Spirit of God had begun to work, and went on patiently working for the next five years.

* * * * *

He had been going through a restless, difficult period, and his mother knew it. A mission was to take place at the Assembly

Rooms in Putney High Street (now W. H. Smith's bookshop), and the speaker was a Miss Maynard, but there was no great enthusiasm on the part of the congregation. Some had felt the time was not ripe for a mission, and the attendance was disappointing; besides, missions conducted by elderly ladies were unorthodox. Nevertheless, Mrs. Pope felt led to urge her fourteen-year-old son to accompany her. He did not wish to go, and only consented on condition that his friend Cecil should go too. So on a damp, misty evening, on April 23rd, 1893, the three set out from their homes in Fulham, and the rather reluctant lads followed the mother right to the second row from the front of the hall, and stared at the unusual little lady on the platform.

She was not the type who would naturally have appealed to boys. She wore a queer bonnet tied under her chin with white strings, and had small sausage curls arranged each side of her forehead. But when the singing was over and she stepped forward with her well-worn open Bible, the bonnet and the curls suddenly ceased to matter. There was power and sweetness in her presentation, and her clear voice rang out through the hall:

"Behold, I stand at the door, and knock. If any man hear My voice, and open the door, I will come in to him, and will sup with him, and he with Me."

She spoke of the Lord knocking at the fast-closed doors of really bad people—the drunkards and the murderers and those who had sunk very low. The clean-living boy from the Christian home knew he was not like that, and he breathed a sigh of relief. But she spoke of other hearts where the Saviour knocked—the people who were so good and so respectable that they saw no need to open the door.

But Dick knew that he was very needy and very restless, and now the old lady seemed to be looking straight at him as she spoke of those who passed for good, decent men and women, but who knew the plague of their own hearts. Very earnestly she appealed to all present to open the door, and then a hymn was given out. All who liked might leave during the singing of that hymn. Any who wished might stay.

> Have you any room for Jesus,
> He Who bore your load of sin?

Nearly everyone was leaving the hall. Dick stood irresolute, and glanced at Cecil. And at that moment his mother leaned across and whispered all the pent-up longing of fourteen years in five words, "Dick, I'm thinking of you".

That finished it. Dick sat down, and found the tears pouring down his cheeks. He was glad the church was practically empty. The hymn was finished, and the tiny speaker had left the platform and was kneeling beside him.

"Dear man," she said quaintly, "do you want to let the Lord Jesus into your heart?"

"I do."

"Then you must tell Him so for yourself. I can't do it for you."

And so Dick prayed. It was a faltering prayer which broke down in the middle, but it reached the Saviour's ear; and now Cecil was kneeling beside him, praying too. Both boys left the hall rejoicing in the knowledge of forgiven sin.

Later in the evening, he was in his bedroom, when there was a knock at the door, and his next eldest sister, Daisy, who had taught him and prayed for him since childhood, came in.

"It's a special day for you, isn't it, Dick?" she said, "Would you mind if we prayed together?"

So they prayed, and she gave him a cardboard-covered text book on which was written 'To Dick from Dai'. There were few reserves in that family. Dick was born again, and they all rejoiced together. The mother's prayers were answered. All her children were Christ's.

There was little else to show for that mission, and years later there was a small paragraph about it in a religious paper:

"May I repeat the story of the campaign held years ago, against the wishes of some of the church members? From all human standpoints it was a failure. The only visible result was the conversion of a fourteen-year-old boy. His name? Richard Hudson Pope."

The account was inaccurate, for Cecil was also converted, but it illustrates in a remarkable way what R. H. P. often said later on:

"It sometimes takes a whole mission to save one child. I notice, looking back over the years, how often each mission is the outbringing of one person who goes on and does exploits. I do not mean that others do not stand, but often there is one who outstands, and it looks as though God allowed a great effort in order to win one—joy in the presence of the angels over *one*."

And now, at the outset of his Christian life, his parents were still his closest spiritual counsellors, and remained so as long as they lived. He could never overestimate their influence, and, as an old man, he could not speak of them without emotion. There were so many precious memories; there was that morning when he was sixteen years old, dressing immaculately for his first job, when his father slipped into the room. "Dick," he said, "things are going to be a bit different now. Shall we pray together?"

There was the bright morning of his marriage, when his mother came to him early, and kneeling beside her son, she prayed earnestly for the blessing of the Lord which maketh rich and addeth no sorrow with it. And then there were the last words she ever spoke to him, in 1913. She was seventy-two and she had been ill; she was propped up in bed, holding a sheet of paper in her hand. "Did I ever show you this one, Dick?" she said, and sang a hymn, of which she had written the words and composed the music:

> There's a fight to be fought, there's a race to be run,
> There are dangers to meet by the way.

But the voice was feeble and she sank back exhausted. "I'm glad I haven't got to think it all out now," she said, and later, "I'm just resting on the Rock of Ages, where I've stood all these years..."

There was a pause. "Dick," she said very earnestly, "it's a good thing to be in time. Tell them to be in time—tell them to be in time."

He saw she was tired out, and slipped away with a brief goodbye. He did not know that he would never see her alive again, and those last words became one of the great signposts of his life. More and more as he grew older, his heart would burn as he looked out over the multitudes of clean, merry little faces lifted to his, knowing that every Christless year would draw their feet further away from Him, and stain their lives more deeply. Was it any wonder that he spoke to them urgently of sin and salvation? In his retiring speech he cried:

> "The needs of the older young people are great, but the needs of the little children are greatest: the child converted at ten is not going to become a menace to society at sixteen. We are the *Children's Special Service Mission*. Let us ever remain so!"

CHAPTER TWO

"Dick, You Must Do Something"

THE first time I was introduced to R. H. P. in private life, he was standing in the passage of a boarding house in Bangor, Northern Ireland, cogitating over a letter he had just received from a newly-converted boy of sixteen.

"He says he went to bed on Sunday afternoon because he had nothing to do!" said R. H. P. in tones of incredulous horror! "And it's the same every evening; he finishes work on the farm at 6.30 and then has nothing to do! Nothing to do at sixteen, and a Christian! My reply will leave him in no doubt whatsoever about something to do."

The words "something to do" were perhaps more than any others the keynote of his active life. Though he made doctrines clear to children, he never claimed to be a theologian ("I think it is a very nice verse," he replied equably to a young divinity student who wanted an explanation of some controversial text), nor, as a young man, was he a mystic or a scholar. His love for Christ drove him into steady action, and became the constraining motive of untiring hard work; and once again it was his mother who pointed out to him the path of service, which his young feet followed so eagerly. She brought up the subject within a few hours of his conversion.

"Dick," she said, "now that you are a Christian you must do something."

So they looked round together, and one of his older sisters had a good idea. Every Sunday afternoon she and one of her other brothers walked from Putney to Barnes—a walk of nearly three miles across Barnes Common, but Sunday transport was taboo—to teach in the Sunday school of the Welcome Mission, and Dick could join them. They admitted that he was too young to teach, but he could look after the library, and mind babies, so that burdened little sisters could attend the classes unencumbered.

It was not an attractive form of service for a fourteen-year-old boy. His love for children was quite unawakened at that time, but apparently they loved him. They were dirty, smelly babies, and they crowded on to his lap, and wriggled and fought and dribbled. "There was a horrible little baby called Freddy. He was enough to put me off children for life!" he reminisced many years later. But Freddy was faithfully cared for every Sunday, and on the way home the three stopped at a cottage and held a little service with old Mr. and Mrs. Harding, who were invalids. They had been doing this only for a few months when Mr. Harding died, and Dick saw death for the first time. Gazing in awe at the still face, it was indelibly impressed on him that the time to serve God was very short. He must not waste a moment.

"The earlier you get into it, the sooner you get on," he would say later. "It was not much, but it was a beginning."

He was delivered from the babies by the urgent need for an organist, and, young as he was, he soon found himself training the choir. But Sunday came round only once a week, and he wanted an outlet on weekdays. He began to wonder what could be done at school. He attended St. Mark's School, Chelsea, and his awakened conscience soon became troubled over a matter he had probably hitherto taken for granted. Cheating and cribbing were the order of the day, and no boy had as yet lifted his voice in protest. It was Dick's first battlefield, and he threw himself into the fray with his usual enthusiasm. He and his friend Charles Chadwick, a decent, straight boy, but not then a Christian, founded what was known as 'the Non-Cheating League'. The fourteen-year-old president gave an inauguration address which was typed out for the benefit of members. It was a vigorous document announcing, characteristically, that *something is going to be done*. "We must expect to be laughed at," he pointed out, "and it will be one of the hardest things to bear. The whole road will not be like melted butter, but on the other hand it will not all be like hot bricks." He advised the members not to fight among themselves, and not to force a boy to join against his will, and ended up rather unexpectedly, "Now I must shut up, as I did not mean to write nearly so much."

The League flourished for a time, and even had attractive membership cards printed with the pledge on the front, "I promise by the help of God to keep from cheating in every sense of the word, both at school and elsewhere", and inside was a list of reasons:

1. Because it will injure myself.
2. Because it will injure others.
3. If I cheat in school it will lead to my cheating in business.
4. Because others will not get their right places in class.

And on the back was printed their motto, "Thou God seest me".

But the League petered out after a while, to its president's profound disappointment. Yet he was beginning to learn that every battle for right against wrong is of intrinsic worth in itself, quite apart from its results.

But the Non-Cheating League did have one result. His friend Charles Chadwick was watching him closely during those schoolboy years. Outwardly a good-living boy, he found himself constantly falling short of those Christian standards he so admired in others. Even his friend Dick, so impulsive, and brimming over with fun, seemed to have found some aim in life which he lacked. He was often kept in check by Dick's life. Dick seemed to know where to stop.

The two boys played together in the holidays, never touching on spiritual matters, reserved on the subject of the barrier that lay between them. But one day, Charles was leaving the Popes' garden to go home when he heard running steps behind him, and Dick, very red in the face, caught him up and threw an arm across his friend's shoulders. "Charlie, old chap," he blurted out, "have you accepted Christ as your personal Saviour?"

Both boys were highly embarrassed. "I don't know," replied Charlie, shaking off the detaining arm, "I think so". But for two years the unanswered question persisted, and the boy's restlessness increased.

After leaving school, Charles often spent his Sundays in Dick's home, and every Sunday afternoon Dick invited him to accompany him to the boys' meeting he attended at that time. Charles was excellent at inventing excuses, but at last a day came when he ran out of ideas, and was steered triumphantly into the hall. By the end of that first talk Charles knew that the answer to the old question was no, and he decided to go regularly. The third meeting was particularly attractive because it was led by Norman Bennet, well-known footballer and boys' evangelist.

The last hymn was given out, and the last verse was read out solemnly by the speaker:

> Saviour, I will wait no longer,
> Now to Thee I come!

"Don't sing it unless you really mean it," said Norman Bennet, and a moment later he noticed the silent boy gazing at the words.

"Can I walk home with you?" asked Bennet. It was only a short way, but they paced the streets together for four hours that night. Much of their talk centred on God's standards of Christian living, and at last Charles burst out, "It's just no good talking to me about being a Christian; it is absolutely impossible for me to live like that."

"It certainly is."

"Then if it's impossible, why mock me by talking to me about it?"

"Because 'I can do all things through Christ which strengtheneth me'."

Light dawned, and Dick's old question which had haunted him all those years was answered that night, with joyful assurance. Dick was overjoyed at the news. Sitting in an A.B.C. café opposite Mansion House Station, he wrote a hymn, while consuming hot buttered toast and strawberry jam. He dedicated it to Chadwick, but it rapidly became popular at schoolboy missions and Bible classes.

> Soldier, soldier, fighting in the world's great strife,
> On thyself relying, battling for thy life.
> Trust thyself no longer,
> Lean on Christ, He's stronger!
> I can all things, all things do through Christ which
>   strengtheneth me.

Chadwick's reply is still extant:

"Dear old Dick,

I received this morning the hymn you composed. I cannot express to you how I feel about it, old fellow; for you to do this as a testimony of friendship is quite enough of itself, but when it is all the outcome of the verse which has been more to me than anyone can know, I feel unable to express my thanks. All I can do, with Christ's help, to be worthy of it, I will.

"I have, as you know, had a truly wonderful deliverance from a life that might have drifted from bad to worse until I dread to think what might have been the end, but I can and do praise God today for His great goodness, and I mean to yield my life to Him, and with His aid, we cannot tell how great the service we two fellows may do for Him.

"I'm awfully fond of you, old man . . . goodbye, and God bless you for all you have been and are to me. . . ."

Rich old friendships, which lasted through life! Charles Chadwick later became Assistant Chaplain General in Malta, and won many in the forces to Christ. But at that time they were sixteen-year-old schoolboys, and Dick at least was no less self-opinionated and self-confident than most outwardly successful lads of his age. God was blessing his efforts, and he was not introspective. He decided to link up with some organized Christian campaign during the summer holidays, and set off with Chadwick and Edward Olney (a new friend who later became one of the pioneers of Crusaders' Union) to Llanfairfechan, where Mr. Russell Hill was leading a C.S.S.M.

The boys were too young to take any active part, but they did what they could and learned much. Dick was full of holiday spirits and enthusiasm, and was no doubt a trial at times: one evening he started an argument which finished in an unfriendly manner, and although at first he felt he had got the best of it, it preyed on his mind, and he felt he must write and apologize. "I'm sorry I spoke as I did, but as a matter of fact you were in the wrong," ran the first letter, but here he stopped. "It won't do," he thought. "I must try again." But four letters went into the wastepaper basket before he could bring himself to write a straight letter of apology.

Yes, there was much to learn. There are great dangers in constant activity. It can be a field in which pride, love of the limelight and self-display can flourish; but God had His hand over this young life, and because every moment and every talent was being used in God's service, the Master took His pupil in hand and taught him. A stationary craft cannot be guided, but this vessel was ever on the move—often off-course, sometimes nearly going under, but always pressing forward. The mistakes and setbacks must have seemed tragedies at the time, but looking back, he recognized them for what they were—blessed occasions of learning his own weakness and fallibility, the soil out of which was to grow that strong, simple dependence on the Holy Spirit which characterized him later on.

His sixteenth year was a year of change and conflict. He had come home from school as usual one evening, when his older brother walked in from work and said, "There's a vacancy in the office if Dick comes tomorrow." So next day he set off, and started on the career which was to last for the next seven years—typing, keeping books and accounts in a London office. It was a good opening, but the boy was troubled. He felt he had already been called into full-time work for God, and he wished to be a Baptist minister. Then, as he prayed and sought God's will, an old friend of his mother's wrote offering "to send me to Cambridge University and meet all expenses if I would enter the C. of England ministry". We have his own account of his search for the right decision.

"It was a very hard choice, for I had never thought there was any possibility of a university career for me, and I would have loved it, but after much prayer, thought and study I felt I must refuse the gracious offer, and I think subsequent events have proved that the decision was a right one.

"When I was about seventeen we made application to Spurgeon's College, but were told there would be no vacancy for three years. Here again I can see God's guiding hand at work, for I have come to the conclusion that where a children's evangelist hopes to reach youngsters of various denominations it is better that he should not be ordained to any specific denomination."

But at the time it cost him much, and the mother on whose advice he had always depended now stood back and refused to influence him in any way. She realized that the time had come when he must be guided by his own principles before God alone. He finally refused the first possibility because he felt that he could not conscientiously accept the wording of the infant baptism service. His mother accepted his decision without comment, but shortly after, he sought her out, and told her he wanted to be baptized by immersion.

"Oh, Dick, I'm so glad," she cried. "I've been praying for this ever since your conversion."

So he made his confession of faith at the Putney Baptist Church, and the longing to give more time to God's service grew deeper than ever. But years later, he looked back and thanked God for His restraining discipline.

"The Lord went on with His training," he said. "When I was sixteen years old how I wanted to go and be an evangelist. I thought it would be lovely to float in on the tide and be 'it'. But God said, 'No. You haven't had your training yet', and He put me in a London office to push a pen for seven years. Young business men say, 'All very well for you preachers, you don't know what businessmen have to put up with!'—but I do. It was all in the training, in the making of a man who was going to have a ministry for God. It showed me what men were like; it showed me how wicked I was myself and how prone to fall into sin. It showed me a little bit of what other people were doing, and sometimes people might have shaken their heads and said, 'I wonder if he was ever converted at all'. All the time *I* knew. God knew the time was not then. I think I wanted limelight, and God saw that I was more like a bulb that, in its early stages, needs to be put in the dark. Early development sometimes means early decay. Someone said to me once about a certain person, 'You know, he started his preaching rather soon. He went on all right for a year or two, but now he has spent his tuppence.' It was a funny way of putting it, but I know what it meant. He hadn't much left. He ought to have stored up more first."

Those years in business were years of temptation and sometimes of failure. He began to see no harm in things that he would have condemned earlier on as inconsistent with Christian living, and among other things he began to smoke. His eighteenth and nineteenth years were years of leanness of soul; he might well have undergone a serious spiritual breakdown at this point had it not been for two factors. The first was the well-tried anchor of his mother's prayers and counsel.

"Dick," she said thoughtfully one night, "have you begun to smoke?"

"Yes, Mother, I have," he replied.

There was a pause.

"Dick, do you think you really need it?"

"No, I don't *need* it. Do you mean you would really rather I didn't do it?"

"Well, I think that *is* it."

"Then, Mother, I won't do it any more." And he didn't. It was as simple as that. He had trusted her so implicitly for nineteen years that her lightest wish was still his law.

The second factor was the influence of his friend Edward Olney—another close friendship which lasted throughout their lives. Dick's feet were slipping, but Edward was like a rock. Dick checked his life by the steady, consistent, upright life of his friend, and came to his senses, and back to God. And the new upsurge of repentant love must find outlet in some new form of activity.

Dick was in an insurance office, Olney in a wholesale haberdashery firm, and Chadwick in an office in the South Eastern Railway. Their evenings were free, and Dick, restored, was once again looking round for 'something to do'. With amazing zeal and fearful lack of experience they borrowed the Wardy Street Mission Hall at Earlsfield, and advertised boys' meetings. They decided to attract the boys with drill, but the boys needed no attraction whatsoever, and turned up seventy strong the first night. The hall was too small to carry out their plans for such a number, so they decided to drill twelve at a time. All went well until the elected twelve were standing in a row; then number one fell against number two, and number two against number three, and the line collapsed like a row of joyful ninepins. This was too much for the fifty-eight onlookers; the whole lot pitched in, and a glorious free fight ensued, which ended in the would-be missioners emptying the hall partly by force, partly by persuasion.

The boys had had a wonderful evening and were only too ready to come again. The teachers, in a slightly less confident mood, tried to admit only a limited number. But an urgent knock at the door caused one of them to open it, to be caught full in the nose by a cleverly compounded ball of mud and snow which blackened exactly half his face. The applause nearly brought the roof down and the meeting ended in a joyful riot. On the third evening, there was still not the slightest difficulty in getting the boys in, but someone on the outside filled the lock with slate pencils, so for half an hour no one could get out again.

But if the three lacked experience they possessed an amazing amount of perseverance. "We are going on till we get a meeting," they said, and go on they did. After a time, interest began to flag and fewer boys turned up. They found they could control a smaller number, and great was their joy one night when they persuaded the group to sit quietly and listen to the Word of God.

R. H. P. remembers two who were probably led to Christ through those early efforts, but whatever the results among the boys, the gain to those three earnest, determined young teachers was incalculable. Unknown to themselves, they were training each other, as only true friends, united in a cause, can do. They laughed at each other, they criticized each other. They prayed together, and encouraged each other. And each busy day they were learning, learning, learning, sometimes through gradual success, but mostly through their mistakes.

One incident during those years stands out vividly. His holiday was due, and, as usual, he longed to spend it in service for his Master, so he joined the C.S.S.M. party at Penmaenmawr under the leadership of the Rev. Harold Salmon. He seems to have enjoyed himself immensely, judging from his literary efforts at the time—a whole series of gay jingles, sparkling with puns, nicknames and current jokes; but there was one thing which worried him very much. There was that great sand pulpit he helped to dig every morning; and there was he, bursting with good evangelical matter, and 'Pa' Salmon had never once asked him up into that pulpit to speak. Perhaps it was just an oversight, and he tried to wait patiently, but he felt puzzled and resentful, not knowing how closely the kind, wise eyes of the older man were watching him. Then one morning Mr. Salmon came to Dick's room, not to invite him to speak, but to talk to him about his own spiritual life and about victory over self. They ended on their knees, man and boy together, yielding themselves in deeper consecration to their Lord. Dick's eyes had been opened during that talk, and he was thankful he had not been asked to speak. He recognized that he must go further and stoop lower himself before he could help anyone else.

A little later he was asked to speak, but his self-confidence had deserted him. "It was not much of a pulpit and not much of a sermon," he remarked afterwards. He was learning that his natural fluency, his humour, his talent in dealing with children—even his hard work and zeal in God's service—were simply not enough. That day he seems to have learned it more thoroughly than ever before. "That pulpit," he said, "was a mound of stones. It was the burial place of my pride, but the resurrection place of a hope for future usefulness."

CHAPTER THREE

Comedian and Editor

R. H. P.'s interest in telegraph boys had started one evening, when he and Olney had accompanied Norman Bennet, who was conducting what was then known as 'a mission for roughs'. Only three 'roughs' turned up, so Bennet went out into the streets to compel them to come in. He returned with eight uniformed telegraph boys, and they all enjoyed a good evening. At the close of it, Bennet remarked regretfully, "What a pity there is nothing here for telegraph boys!"

It was a challenge to his two young assistants, who lost little time in finding out that there *was* something for telegraph boys. There was a society known as the Telegraph Messengers Christian Association (T.M.C.A.), and it had been started by Miss Donnisthorne, of Leicester, as a large Sunday afternoon Bible class held in her house. It was a distinctive Bible class, in that each boy took his turn in introducing the subject, and then the meeting was thrown open for discussion. The members were taught to study their Bibles, to witness in their work, and united prayer was made easy for them by the method of 'short, quick telegrams'. Many a boy who could not have prayed at length found he could take part in this way.

The class became a society, originally called 'The Christian Endeavour Society for Telegraph Boys and Junior Postmen', and it spread to other parts of England. There was a flourishing branch in Brighton, and Miss Synge ran the T.M.C.A. institute in Ivy Lane, London. The Association had proved a real blessing to many boys. They wore a badge, and were easily recognized in their various offices. "I am going to get another badge, Miss," said one to Miss Donnisthorne, "and then I can have one on each coat. I couldn't be without it at the Post Office; it has been such a help to me so many times when I'm tempted. The sight of the badge seems to pull me up."

One of the senior postmen remarked, "There is no difficulty in knowing who are the Christians. They are always cheery, and their influence is felt right through the office."

The institute in Ivy Lane was the perfect setting for R. H. P., and he spent most of his spare time furthering its welfare, while Olney started another branch in the Borough. Miss Synge seems to have been a wise, kind trainer of workers, encouraging and sometimes criticizing her young helpers in their speaking. It was an organization in which all his gifts could be used unstintingly, and where he found full scope for his remarkable versatility—his music, his organizing and dramatic ability, his humour and his literary talent—all could be used (and how he enjoyed using them!) for Christ and the boys.

Many were the gay entertainments and sing-songs he organized, and the boys loved him. He dramatized Pickwick Papers, wrote comic songs, organized rallies, and glimpses of these happy evenings appear in the local papers of the day, for R. H. P.'s fame was beginning to spread in the district.

The *Daily News* had the following report:

"Of all the three hundred or so May meetings, none, it is safe to say, will be of a more lively nature than the annual gathering of the T.M.C.A. which took place last evening at Exeter Hall. Imagine that grave building thronged with merry-eyed, active lads full of exuberant spirits, bent on passing the time and showing their appreciation of everything by stamping their feet, by excessive shouting, whistling and cat-calls, and it will be seen that anything more unlike an ordinary May meeting cannot be imagined. Yet these same lads, when Mr. Talbot Rice offered prayer, stood silent with heads bowed, and joined in the Lord's Prayer."

From another paper:

"On May 9th an evening of recitals and songs were given by Messenger J. M. Beill, and an address by Mr. Pope. The last-named gentleman proved himself to be very useful. He played the piano, recited, sang, and gave a very practical temperance address."

Happy, exuberant days! Rhymes flowed from his pen. There were "Pope's Parodies Lost", of which one example was:

> What means this great bald patch?
>   Robin 'ad 'air!
> Now he has lost his thatch,
>   Robin 'ad 'air!

and there was the rollicking operetta with its song about the Sea-Serpent.

> Oh, can't the Captain tell some tales, my boy, my boy.
> Just hear his song of a serpent long, ahoy, ahoy.
> Its head was on American shore, its tail in Timbuctoo;
> You can't believe a word he says! I'm sure I can't—can you?

He was noted too for his comic solo performances, and no doubt these things attracted many boys, but although the spiritual side was certainly not neglected, the balance was going wrong, and a night came when God spoke to him about it all. He did not give up his entertainments, but he realized that once again self must be kept firmly in check. He spoke of this experience many years later.

> "You would not have believed, would you, that I used to do entertainments at parties and things. I was the 'funny man'. They were entertainments you could not take exception to; I don't apologize for them, but one night a boy said to me, 'Mother was at the entertainment last night. Oh, Mr. Pope, first Mother laughed till she cried, then she laughed till her nose bled, then she couldn't laugh any more!' I don't think I needed to say 'I'm sorry I've done these things', but one day God spoke to me. 'If you are going to be known as a comedian you are not going to be known as a holy man. People don't come to a comedian if they are in trouble about their souls.' One night I had been speaking at a boys' meeting, and we had had a very solemn time. After the meeting was over, I was singing a funny song at the harmonium and everyone was laughing. I was just going on when there was a knock, and the door opened. I called out 'Come in,' and a voice said, 'Sir, have I got to be very sorry for my sins before I come to Christ?' I left the boys and the organ, but I was in no mood to talk to that boy, and he never made a very satisfactory Christian. God had told me to let something go, and I had been disobedient."

And yet right from the first the 'comedian' was carrying on a fruitful spiritual ministry, as further newspaper reports show.

> "We shall not soon forget the social hour after the service on Sunday evening, February 16th. A hundred lads and younger men were present. Simple refreshments were provided, some music and two earnest addresses by Mr. Bone and Mr. Pope. A great many stayed to the after-meeting and a good number definitely decided for Christ and went home rejoicing. They have since given unmistakable evidence that the work is real. This shows that lads can be reached, and perhaps there is no more urgent call than this on behalf of the

lads; in Mr. Pope we seem to have a man with a perfect genius for dealing with them. What an inestimable blessing it would be if such a man could devote all his time to this formative period."

He was an ardent contributor to the *Boy's Mail-Bag* too—the T.M.C.A. periodical—and soon became its editor. The rallies he organized must have been a highlight in the life of every lad who attended. They poured in from Bristol, Bath, Cheltenham, Malvern, Reading, Aberdeen, Dundee, Biggleswade, Cambridge, Chatham, Ipswich and Dover, and all round London, over a thousand strong, and united in R. H. P.'s song composed for the occasion:

> Our unique association
> Deserves the approbation
> Of all who wish their country well.
> For we offer education,
> Harmless fun and recreation,
> And other things too numerous to tell.
> But there's something greater still
> We are striving to fulfil
> That Messengers in truth and honour know.
> If you win a fellow's heart
> You have made a proper start,
> It is bound to help the G.P.O.

There were expeditions to see the sights of London, games and entertainments, and solemn, memorable meetings which bore fruit. Many went back to their jobs strengthened and confirmed in the Christian life. Others found Christ and went back to witness in the difficult surroundings of the G.P.O.—just how difficult, the following letter shows:

"Sir, hoping this letter will find you quite well, as it leaves me at present. I am very sorry I caused a disturbance Monday. One of the Messengers has turned a Christian, but I don't think he will keep so long. His name is Buddle. *Later*. I've seen Buddle and he says he is still holding on, though he has to put up with a lot of sneers. They keep on at the poor boy all day long, and when they have got his temper up he says, Down with Satan, and then he lays his head on the table and has a word of prayer. I will close with love from all the Messengers of Dover x x x ."

The old premises at Ivy Lane had long become far too small to house the members, and new headquarters were rented at 4

Mitre Court, Cheapside. Here, in a roomy gymnasium, the opening ceremony took place with an entertainment and (of course) a song composed for the occasion by Mr. Pope. It consisted of ten verses, but the first gives the gist of it:

> We've all been talking long and loud
>   About our great desirements;
> At least we've lighted on a place
>   That well suits our requirements;
> And though we're loth to leave the spot
>   We've shared so many joys in,
> It's no use having Institutes
>   You cannot get the boys in.

The Lord Mayor and Lady Mayoress presided on this occasion, and the work in its spacious new premises grew by leaps and bounds; and at the same time there was growing in Dick's heart a strong desire to be free of the office, and to give his life to evangelizing boys.

> "I felt that in all this," he wrote, "God was drawing me away from the idea of a ministerial life to that of an evangelist among boys. And thus He led me on. The discipline of the office routine, learning obedience, punctuality and hard work, rubbing shoulders with unsaved people, and finding out what a Christian life calls for in a busy, self-seeking world, gaining experience—all these things were needed to make up my training, without which I do not think I could have undertaken the work of an evangelist. To come in, as an evangelist does, on the top of the tide, as it were, and sail along for ten days or so, is likely to make him under-value the steady settled-down work which has led up to the mission, and will have to continue. Part of his preparation for the peculiar life of the evangelist should be to do settled-down work, and to learn by experience what it means to prepare for a mission, and the hard work, and sometimes the heart-breaking work, of the 'follow up'."

And then suddenly, in 1902, when Dick was twenty-three, a gentleman named D. M. Panton, editor of a Christian magazine, who had no doubt been reading the local newspaper reports with interest, accosted the young man. "Would you have time to come down to my club and dine with me?" he asked.

Wondering, Dick presented himself, and over their dinner Mr. Panton explained the purpose of his invitation. He was in touch with a social settlement in Ipswich, and they needed a warden. Would Dick be willing to go?

He was a young man for the job, and had little experience of rough, down-and-out men. Yet he felt it was the first step out toward full-time evangelistic work, and he accepted. It was a big wrench to part from his telegraph messengers, and his farewell letter to them summed up all his desire for them during the years he had served them. Here is part of what he wrote:

"Now, fellows, as a parting word, remember 'Jesus Christ, the same yesterday, today and for ever'. Friends go, associations are severed, things change, and we along with them, but though heaven and earth pass away, Christ and His Word will not pass away. Stick to Him and that Word of His, and you may be sure of this, for He Himself says it, 'Lo, I am with you always, even unto the end of the world', and provided the Lord Jesus is with us, everything else will take its right place—joys, troubles, and difficulties—for 'with Christ in the vessel we smile at the storm'.

"Rest in this fact, that if you are a Christian, not only are you holding on to Christ, but God is holding on to you, and your standing does not depend on your feeble grasp, but on the strong hand of your Father—as the psalmist says, 'Let Thy hand be upon the man of Thy right hand'."

In the year that followed he may sometimes have had cause to wonder at the leading of his Father's hand, for he was guided from the peak of success and popularity into what must have seemed, at times, a valley of humiliation. But

> "The flowers need night's cool darkness,
> The moonlight and the dew"

and there were streams and wells in that valley; a fresh acceptance of his limitations, a new dependence on Christ; it was a passage-way, from which he emerged a humbler, steadier man, ready to travel straight ahead towards his life's goal.

CHAPTER FOUR

"I Didn't Shine all the Time"

THERE is little information to be gathered about the year when R. H. P. worked as Warden at the men's social settlement. The appointment was not an easy one for a young man; age and experience were needed, and while he could hold boys by his personality and oratory, he did not have the same effect on the type of man who frequented the settlement. There were problems of discipline, behaviour, beyond his power to cope with, for outside his natural environment of boys and children he was a shy man, and never quite at his best with adults. The appointment ended within a year, when the work of Warden and Secretary were combined in one older, more experienced leader.

Nevertheless one soul was saved at the settlement that year—that of a boy who was to carry the Gospel to thousands of children in years to come. William Charles Knights, who became one of the pioneers of the Caravan Mission to Village Children, was wandering through Ipswich one Sunday afternoon when he saw a notice on the door of the social settlement.

> Come to a men's meeting
> on Sunday at 8 p.m.
> Speaker: R. Hudson Pope
> All MEN are welcome

William was only a boy, but he worked in the foundry and earned a man's wage, so he walked in and found just one empty seat in the hall where he could sit, well hidden behind the stove. There, for the first time in his life, he heard the very words that had drawn Dick to the Saviour nine years previously, "Behold, I stand at the door, and knock. If any man hear My voice, and open the door, I will come in . . ."

William did not hear one word of the address—he was held by that verse. But at the close of the meeting an appeal was given, followed by the invitation, "If anyone wants to come to the Saviour, will he come and have a chat with me in the warden's room?"—and William was at the door in a trice. The transaction with God had already taken place in that corner behind the stove, as the boy's radiant face testified, but they talked and prayed, and he promised to come again the following Sunday. He kept his word and returned with his first convert, his workmate Jim Fraser, whom he had led to Christ during the week.

During the meeting, Mr. Pope asked William if he would like to give his testimony, and we have his own account of what followed:

"Up I jumped and began talking for, and of, my Lord and Saviour Jesus Christ. Afterward the Rev. T. Carrot invited me to give the same talk in his weeknight meeting. He spent much time inviting his people to come, and they came. The hall was full, and the Holy Spirit was with us, and God blessed His Word. At the close of the meeting Mr. Pratt, Warden of the Sailors' Mission, invited me to preach. 'Sir,' I said, 'I have never preached a sermon in my life, but I will come to tell about my Lord Jesus Christ and what He has done for me and will do for others.' 'That's it,' he said, 'that's just what I want.' True to promise, I arrived at the Mission at 5.45 p.m. and was confronted by a huge notice on the door:

COME AND HEAR
WILLIAM KNIGHTS
THE BOY PREACHER
TONIGHT AT 6 P.M.
ALL SEATS FREE—COME."

They came, and filled the hall, and the boy's reputation was established. He received invitations from all over the district, and four years later he left the foundries and formed his life-long association with the Caravan Mission. Fifty-six years later he was able to write "I cannot remember holding a mission without results. Here a little, there much revival blessing."

So that difficult year was not without fruit, nor without valuable experience. R. H. P. worked desperately hard to reclaim some of the men among whom he worked, and often got little thanks for his pains. He turned up one day with a black eye after a fight with a drunk, and his eyes were opened to the misery and poverty and drunkenness that existed in the slums at the beginning of the century. But in his spare moments he turned back with relief and gratitude to the comparative innocence of childhood. This new knowledge of the degradation of sin made him long more than ever before to save the children, to set their feet on the road to heaven before they had strayed so far, and stained and soiled their lives irrevocably. So during the time when he held his appointment at the men's settlement, he also founded a ragged boys' school, a telegraph boys' class, and a Boys' Brigade Company. It was hardly surprising that, when his year was up and his resignation handed in, he should step straight into the post of Warden of a boys' home in Ipswich.

He had already made his name as a boys' man for the town. William Knights' witness in the foundries alone had brought R. H. P. into close contact with the working lads of the district. It had all started the morning after William's conversion, when he dropped a load of wood on his foot, and instead of swearing and cursing, he had broken out into song. His mate had scoffed at him, but a few weeks later that mate was taken very ill. William took Dick Pope to visit him as he lay dying, and the boy turned to Christ just before his death. In their trials, their imprisonments, and at their death-beds R. H. P. was there. The police were constantly sending for him, and the boys themselves flocked to him; all the social services knew him and appealed to him. Any boy in need, whether physically, mentally or spiritually, could claim his help, and find it poured out on him freely, lovingly, unstintingly.

The Boys' Home was a new social venture, and an account of its purpose and proposed activities was published in the *East Anglian Times* in 1903.

"When a boy is starting life as a wage-earner he has reached a most important period of his existence, and his parents, at such a time, watch every turn of his thoughts and actions, and study his budding aspirations. His expanding frame will be fed as well as circumstances will allow . . . but there are unfortunately many boys who lack the thoughtful attention to their mental and physical requirements which the boy with a good home receives. Perhaps they have no parents, or maybe their parents are from the undesirable class. Such boys are found in every town, and it is to be feared that the various benevolent agencies that touch juvenile life do not quite make up the deficiency in the home life of these lads. The only organization that can effectively supply what is needed is such an institution which Ipswich possesses in the Working Boy's Home. This most deserving Home has been carried on since 1899, when it was founded by a small group of benevolent persons. Hitherto the total capacity has been thirteen beds, but now the Home makes a fresh start under greatly improved conditions at 20 Church Street, and the Committee have been fortunate in securing the services, as Warden of the new Home, of Mr. R. Hudson Pope, who has been for some time past the resident Warden of the Social Settlement."

A detailed description of the new building follows. The boys had been given "the benefit of the most tasteful decoration—in their library, dining-room, games room and sleeping accommodation". It then hastens to assure any of the old school of thought that "while the Committee provide the boys with every comfort, it very properly avoids surrounding them with luxuries which would be out of keeping with their future life".

It was a good, up-to-date venture, and they had found a good man to run it. The warden's work was described as follows: "The work of the warden among boys will not be confined within the walls of the Home. He will interest himself generally in any societies in the town dealing with boys, where his services have been requisitioned. He will keep a register of suitable lodgings for boys for the benefit of those leaving the Home, or others outside who care to take advantage. The Committee will strictly avoid doing anything that would relieve parents of their responsibility, and will not accept boys whose parents are able to support them. It should also be understood that the Committee do not intend to do anything that will induce boys to leave the country and take up work in the town."

The Home was opened on December 8th, 1903, and once again a lively account appeared in the local paper.

"To accommodate the visitors a marquee had been erected, and was filled to overflowing. The reading room with which it was connected, and which had for the occasion been enlarged by the removal of the partition separating it from the Warden's room, was charmingly adorned with flowers and brilliantly lighted, while huge fires blazed in the fire-places, over one of which was carved 'Home, sweet home, there's no place like home'. The ceremony was fixed for 3.30 p.m., but it was quite half an hour after that time before Lady Beatrice arrived on the scene. Nevertheless she was heartily applauded when she arose and hoped that the Home would prosper and that there would never be a vacant bed. She was followed by Mrs. John Cobbold, who also said her say. She said that when they sent their sons away to school they should think of the boys sent out into the world practically without a friend, and without anything to encourage them to do well. The work of errand boys was surely very hard. They received much scolding and little praise. They preyed on their orchards, she knew, and got through their hedges, but had they any outlet for those delightful animal spirits which were considered so charming in the sons of their hearers? She thought Mr. Pope would give them a better prospect."

The speeches that followed reflect the social problems of the age. One said:

"It used to be a matter of voluntary effort to educate a child at all, and when a child was educated, the effort was over. The boy passed out as a young worker, part of a working family. But the State has now taken in hand the education of the children, and the dangerous time now was when a boy left school, and might start working for some large factory or company where any individual interest in his welfare apart from his work was almost impossible. But in this Home he would have the advantage of fatherly care."

Speech followed speech, and all were delighted with the grace and kindness of Lady Beatrice, if not with her punctuality. Donations were mentioned. The Mayoress had promised a bagatelle board, and her youngest son two sets of draughts. Much was said of character-training and the power of sympathy, and the vicar spoke in general terms about the importance of spiritual welfare. R. H. P.'s closing words must have made the company sit up. There was nothing vague about his remarks. He was out to save souls, and he said so.

So the boys arrived, and Ipswich rallied round, and that first Christmas, a fortnight later, must have been a happy one indeed, when, after a Christmas service, the boys repaired to the Corn Exchange to act as waiters to the poor children's Christmas dinner. Then 'walks abroad' till 4.30, when a seasonable repast was served in the Home and presents distributed—oranges and nuts from the Mayoress, cards and crackers, six handkerchiefs, a prayer-book and a pair of shoes all round from various kind ladies; a turkey, a plum pudding, a ham, and last but not least, a Bible apiece donated by thirteen schoolboys in the town.

So the work began and R. H. P. became father to twenty-five lads, some from the workhouse, some from the streets, and some sent by their parents, but none with a home fit to go to. Nor did he in the least confine his activities to the Home. He also continued to run a ragged school, a telegraph boys' class, and a Boys' Brigade. More and more, the police were enlisting his help to cope with juvenile delinquency. He sought suitable work for the boys, and looked carefully into the causes of their condition, often voluntarily taking over the work of the modern probation officer. Nor did he hesitate to attack practices which he felt might tempt or stumble them. After dealing with the case of a boy who had stolen chocolate on Sunday, he wrote a most vehement letter to the local paper condemning the practice of keeping shops open on Sunday. He, too, was largely responsible for the appointment of a sub-committee to enquire into the local conditions of child labour in the streets of the town.

There was no doubt about it, his boys loved him, and many were blessed spiritually. The daily humdrum routine of running a Home and the maintenance of discipline were not matters which came easily to him, and he was often exploited. But there was no one like him for organizing an occasion, and those warm, bright evenings, compounded of fun and laughter and living, loving, teaching, must have made an indelible impression on these homeless, unwanted lads—and his own group were merely the nucleus. His aim was to reach all and any; he issued the following in the local paper:

> "During the coming winter it is our purpose to cater in every possible way for the working boys in Ipswich. We are arranging Saturday evening concerts and lectures and many other attractions which we hope will help to lift our boys, in some measure, out of the sin and misery and degradation of a constant street perambulation into the higher atmosphere of knowledge and a feeling that someone cares whether they are happy or not."

There are reports of special missions, and a memorable evening when Mr. Will Thomas gave his life-story. For, eight years ago, he had tramped into Ipswich penniless, and was converted at a lodging-house meeting, and had become eventually the manager of a large firm of contractors. The boys were deeply impressed, and the meetings grew to overflowing; there were concerts, lectures, talks on 'girls', an invitation to 'the worst boys in Ipswich', followed by another to 'the best boys in Ipswich'. Two hundred under-twelves would meet week by week at 6 p.m., and 250 to 300 over-twelves at 7.30 p.m. for R. H. P.'s Bible class. The town was amazed.

He held parents' meetings too. "Don't leave it to someone else to lead your children to Christ," he urged them. "Have you spoken to them yourselves?" At the close of the meeting he found a troubled woman waiting for him at the door. "I've had Leslie thirteen years," she confessed, "and I've never spoken to him about the Lord. I'll go home and see if he's awake now." Leslie was still awake, and his mother led him to Christ that night. It was the beginning of a long, useful life in the Master's service; in fact, at the time of writing, old Mr. Leslie Leyton is still visiting invalids with Gospel tape recordings.

Many old misspelt letters testify to R. H. P.'s influence. One note from a boy at the Home to his Sunday school teacher, giving a vivid picture of life at 20 Church Street, says:

"Dear Mrs. Woods, I am now taking the pleasure of writing these few lines hoping to find you well as it leaves me the same we are having a jolly time here now there have been Willie, Harry, Charles and West converted in one night, and Willie has a smile now that won't come off. I am serving an apprenticeship with a carpenter, my master is also on the way to Glory, but my Headmaster is carpentering as the Lord Jesus Christ . . . Mr. Pope, our second master, has got a fine Brigade and his band is now being completed with drums etc. We are holding special prayer meetings for the Ipswich working boys which all are welcome in, and may God bless our warden Mr. H. Pope and may he bring more souls to Christ.

> It was a very happy night and no mistake
> When Jesus from my heart did take
> He took the sin that made it ache
> And filled my heart with joy."

There is another, from a boy rejoicing in salvation:

"I like to tell you I stepped over the line at 4 o'clock this afternoon. I have been thinking about it a long while but I have left off thinking and gone over the line. I have heard you and Lietuenant Carrit and Knights talk about it and you three together have led me over the line into the narrow pathway. . . . Yours, over the line, private A. Vale.

P.s.
> Alfred Vale is my name
> England is my nation
> Ipswich is my dwelling place
> And Christ is my salvation."

R. H. P. had the same old team behind him throughout— Charles Chadwick, Harry Carrit, William Knights, fast growing in grace, and Ted Olney. They joined him whenever they could, and Olney's friendship, as ever, was one of the strongest, steadiest influences in his young life, checking his exuberances, keeping his feet on the earth. A lad who had been for months in Olney's embryo Crusader Class, taught and prayed over, was finally converted at one of R. H. P.'s boys' rallies. Dick's joy overflowed.

"Another star in my crown!" he burst out, over a cup of coffee, in the restaurant where they had gone to celebrate.

Olney exploded. "You old star-snatcher!" he stormed. "Who has prayed over him and taught him for months? Who brought him to the rally?—your crown indeed!"

But the love between them was deep and strong, and the shy Olney was drawn out by R. H. P.'s enthusiasm, and each recognized the debt they owed the other. The disappointments and deceptions inevitable in such work would have been almost too much for Olney's sensitive young spirit without R. H. P.'s buoyancy, as current letters reveal:

"Dear Dick.... Was awfully upset on Saturday. The head Inspector came to see me and tell me about X, apparently a Christian—spoke while I was away—had been watched for a year in suspicious places at night. Came up early on Saturday to help and I had to send him off then and there... I never longed for you so much as on Saturday. Had I let myself go, I should have collapsed and cried like a child.

"Now, Dick—you have often said how grand it would be if we could work together for good. I am praying for that night and day, and am preparing as well as I can for the answer. I have pretty nearly thrown over fiction, and am reading the Bible and helpful books when time occurs. I feel more and more convinced that I am not to be a 'city man', and pray daily to be out of it into the real work. I don't see how it can be, but if it is His purpose, He can open up the way. Pray for me, Dick, as I pray for you, and write to me sometimes! I have no pal to talk to, and it is lonely... and don't think this is a sentimental outburst, such as one sometimes gets after good times, but believe it to be, as it is, my greatest desire, and one that has stood the test of years already."

Of what had they dreamed? From all accounts, the boys' work in Ipswich was prospering, and the Home was running well. With a fellow-worker like Olney, there is no telling what they might have achieved together. It is therefore with a sense of surprise that one comes upon the following entry in the *East Anglian Journal* in 1906.

"After much thought and deliberation it has been decided not to renew Mr. Pope's engagement as warden and missioner, which accordingly terminated on December 31st last. It is with deepest regret that the Committee dispense with the services of this gentleman, and they desire to place on record their appreciation of the thorough, energetic way he has carried out his duties, and of the kindly Christian influence he has exercised among the lads. They feel certain Mr. Pope will be remembered as a friend by hundreds of Ipswich boys."

Why, one wonders! Was the pace a little too fast and hot for the titled patrons of the Home, and were they getting a little more than they bargained for? We do not know, but we do know that God's hand was over R. H. P. and his loyal, devoted helpers, leading them each into separate service. Harry Carrit went as a missionary to China, Charles Chadwick enlisted as a chaplain in the Army, William Knights joined the Caravan Mission to Village Children, Olney put all his energies into his Crusader Class, and Dick stepped out into his new appointment with the C.S.S.M.

He was happy and sure of his leading. He had learned by experience that his life-work was not to be as Warden of a Working Boys' Home, and there was much in the past three years that had humbled him and shaken his self-confidence, but that again was all part of the training. He summed it up years later—his own soul's history, as opposed to the glowing newspaper reports, the crowded halls, and the real lasting results in the lives of many boys— "There was not much work for God . . . I didn't shine all the time . . . it wasn't constant . . . it might have been said many times, 'He held on'."

CHAPTER FIVE

On Trial with the C.S.S.M.

R. H. P.'s connection with the Children's Special Service Mission, as has been already mentioned, dated back to 1888, when he attended Mr. Edwin Arrowsmith's mission at Eastbourne, as a child of nine. He had helped at Llanfairfechan, Penmaenmawr and Felixstowe, and already had acquired something of a reputation in C.S.S.M. circles. This was brought home to him when, as a young staff worker, he was introduced to an elderly lady who helped to lead a beach mission. She greeted him as follows: "I've wanted to meet you for a long time, but I've had severe misgivings as to how we should get on!"

There was nothing dramatic about the next step, nor any specific 'call'. The founder of the C.S.S.M., Josiah Spiers, received his 'call' one sunny morning on the beach at Llandudno when he made a text in the sand and gathered a small group of children round it and talked to them. In the same way, R. H. P.'s 'call' to whole-time evangelism among children came from the upturned faces of boys, from their rapt attention night after night, as he spoke to them, in his inimitable way, of the love of Christ. Everyday routine must no longer bind him. He knew now that he must be free for this and this alone.

He was growing in spirit too, reaching up to the light, hungry and thirsty for more of his Lord. Was there a gift that would bring to him the power in service and the victory over sin that he craved for? As usual, he poured out his longings and experiences to the steady Ted Olney, who, in his own quiet way was also hungering for a deeper knowledge of Christ. Had they missed some important doctrine, or would some new truth satisfy them?

"Maybe there is some deeper truth or experience that we have missed so far," said Olney. "If so, we had better ask for it."

So R. H. P., on the verge of his life's work, did as Olney

advised, and prayed earnestly that if there was anything lacking the Lord would give it then and there.

Nothing happened; only a quiet consciousness that there was nothing lacking in Christ, and Christ would manifest Himself to the heart that loved Him and obeyed Him. And with a sense of deep peace and relief the young man was drawn back from these spiritual explorations into the old paths of learning to know Christ through obedient, unstinting service. He never again turned aside from that path, or sought to know his Master by other means. From that day to the end of his active life his attitude was the same.

> Dismiss me not Thy service, Lord,
> But train me for Thy will. . . .
> And I will ask for no reward
> Except to serve Thee still.

So when Mr. Cutting, hearing that he was seeking fresh employment, suggested an interview with the committee of the C.S.S.M., he accepted with no great sense of destiny. In fact he felt very nervous indeed, and imagined a searing examination ahead. But, sitting in the old London office of the C.S.S.M. in Warwick Lane with Mr. Tom Bishop and Mr. George Goodman, his fears somehow melted away. Very few questions were asked in any case (they had probably all been asked before). "We talked of our love for the Lord and for the children," said R. H. P. later, "of our experiences of His saving grace in our own lives, of our love for, and reliance upon, the Word of God, and we prayed together." He was then asked to start work on January 1st, 1906, for a trial period of six months. He was to arrange his own missions, and receive a salary of £150 a year. He stipulated that he only felt qualified to teach boys, but his stipulation was firmly refused. "Mr. Pope," he was told gravely, "you must remember that little girls have souls as well."

The six months passed quickly and both parties were well satisfied; R. H. P. signed his permanent agreement, which stretched on into fifty-four years of unbroken service to God and the C.S.S.M. In those first years he often helped at missions, rather than conducting them, and in consequence learned a great deal from others. He joined young William Knights in his caravan, and worked with Mr. Edmund Clark at the beach mission at Southsea. It was here he met, for the first time, a slim young curate with a black moustache named Guy King, and formed another friendship which lasted through life.

There were two great highlights in his early training. While he was helping at the Surrey Caravan Mission Mr. George Goodman came and held a week of meetings for children. His logical, clear-cut presentation of the Gospel gripped and humbled R. H. P. Night after night he sat quietly listening and learning, and at the end of the week he went and tore up most of his own carefully prepared addresses. "They've seemed all right so far, but they're not much good," he mused beside his bulging wastepaper basket. "There's something in that man's presentation of the Gospel that I haven't got. God helping me, I'll start again."

It was the crystal clarity of divine truth that he aimed at, and about this time he started constructing those models which he must have used hundreds of times over—the bridge from Sinland to Salvationland, King Self's Castle, the envelope addressed to Heaven, and many others. At first there were plenty of hitches, but he perfected them gradually. "Do be careful that your models slide in and out at the right moment," he would warn young evangelists. "I remember saying, 'So, children, you see . . .' and then they didn't see, and then I got all hot and bothered."

The second great milestone in his own education was a lecture given by the headmaster of a school in Birmingham to Sunday school teachers. What R. H. P. heard that day so coloured the atmosphere of all his subsequent missions that it seems worth reproducing it in full.

1. To be in time means to be before time.
2. Children usually do what they know they are expected to do. They hear a whistle and they know they've all got to be quiet. The reason why they don't do what they ought to do is because they don't know what they are expected to do. If you want them to put down their books at the end of a hymn, tell them before the hymn finishes what you want them to do. Stop before the last verse and say something like this: "We shall all put our hymn-books on the bookrest and sit down and take our Bibles." The moment the hymn is over, they will know exactly what to do. If nothing like this is done, half of them will already have done the wrong thing. Or, for instance, "At the close of this hymn we shall remain standing for prayer".

3. Be careful always to give a caution word. Don't suddenly shout out "Stand". Do as the man does in the Army—Atten... shun. Say, "Everybody... stand"; or "Girls only... stand"; and then give them time to do it. Not, "Everybody stand—Tommy, you aren't standing up. Oh, come, Tommy, Tommy."
4. Remember that you are in front of the child, and as you speak to the child you are the wrong way round as it were, and if you say to the children, "I want you all to look to the right", you yourself must look to the left. If you don't, they will look in the wrong direction. If you say, "Hold up your right hand", you must hold your left hand up.
5. Then there is the question of prayer. I always like to say to the children, "When we pray we usually shut our eyes; not because we could not pray with our eyes open. For instance, you may need to pray with your eyes open sometimes, when you are in the playground, or when the teacher is doing a sum on the board (if you shut your eyes you will miss what the teacher is doing). But when we shut our eyes, we shut out other things. I shall shut mine, and I shall trust you to shut yours. The teachers will all do the same. Everybody . . . eyes shut." Don't open your eyes if you have said you aren't going to. Usually the children can be trusted. I was in a meeting once, and the speaker was going to pray, when he stopped suddenly and said, "Sit up, John. I can see you. Don't forget, I can watch as well as pray!" He should not have said it like that.
6. Don't say, "Shall we?" It is, "We shall". The child is there to be told what to do. I was once in a roomful of boys, and we were just going to pray, and I said, "Now, shall we pray?" And a voice from far back of the hall said, "No, we won't!" There was a worse one than that. Dead silence reigned, and we were about to begin to pray when a boy called out in a monotone: "Let us bray"!
7. If you want books passed along, don't suddenly say, "Pass your books to the end of the row", because you have told them to pass before they know what or where. Say something like this: "Hymn books—to the end of the row, pass."
8. Don't make threats you cannot carry out. (Often it is not so much the threat as the boy you cannot carry out!)
9. When you pray at the end of an address, and you know that the

probability is that the moment the address finishes there will be a restlessness, how are you going to prevent it? Just as I am coming to the end of the address, without saying that we are actually at the end, I say, "No, just stay where you are sitting; don't move, anybody. Just as you are sitting now, everybody—eyes shut, and we will close in prayer."

That first year, 1906, saw twenty-four missions, each lasting from a week to a fortnight, and the invitations came in thick and fast. His plan was to work in with the Sunday schools and churches, and he left the preparation of his missions to the teachers. His ministry was to be used by the Holy Spirit to light that spark that would kindle the fuel that had probably been patiently laid for years—to lead the well-instructed children to Christ, and then to hand them back to their own teachers for subsequent building up and Christian fellowship. He went wherever invited, regardless of the size or denomination of the body in question, and, in the early years at least, very seldom refused a request for help.

"I always pray for guidance about whom to refuse," said an over-burdened missioner.

"I ask guidance for who invites me," replied R. H. P.

The aim of his missions was always the same, and remained the same throughout his life. "The job of an evangelist is not to indoctrinate or teach. It is to bring children to Christ," he averred. "If they have never heard the full Gospel they will hear it tonight." They did hear and they did come to Christ. He almost invariably saw results because he expected to see them.

He had his bad moments. He remembers trying to teach a new chorus to a hall full of little toughs. "Oh, what a Saviour!" the chorus ended, and they sang it with gusto. "Now," said R. H. P., "after the word 'oh' I'll raise my hand for silence; then—altogether—'WHAT A SAVIOUR!" He raised his hand . . . dead silence, suddenly broken by a little voice "'e don't 'alf make me laff!" and the meeting relapsed into shouts of mirth. But the bad moments passed quickly, and there were very few meetings that did not end in an atmosphere of tender, loving solemnity.

Many of the early missions were held among very poor children, with their correspondingly sordid backgrounds. They flocked in from the Lancashire mills and factories, from their newspaper rounds and street crossings, from basement kitchens—little white-faced denizens of the slums, drawn from the mud of the streets and squalor of home into the light and warmth and love and laughter of the mission hall. The joyful presence of R. H. P. drew them irresistibly, as the current letters testify. To them he was happiness personified.

"We have enjoyed your meetings—they have been so merry."

"Would it be inconvenient to meet us four boys at the top of Churchfield Road at 4.15 and go for a walk, because you are such a happy, jolly servant of Christ."

"Mother is coming to the mission. I told her how cheerful it was, and now she wants to come."

"The seats are so nice to sit on ... I have brought myself to Christ just as you said at that happy meeting for children."

The letters poured in; over a hundred were received after a mission in Liverpool—little scribbled, misspelt notes on the back of handbills, on ragged shreds of wrapping paper, on sheets torn from exercise books, addressed indiscriminately to Mr. Pope, Mr. Pop, Mr. Pock, Mr. Pape or plain Pope, and signed in the most original ways:

"Your truthful servant of God, Ethel."
"Your dear friend, Willie."
"From the greatest sinner in the world, Mabel."
"I am now one of the lambs of Christ, from a going-to-be true believer, Ethel."
"Remaining no longer a sinner, Lily."
"From a star in your crown for ever, John."
"With love from the boy who is 7½ at Brooklyn Villa."
"From one of your little sheep, Ellen."
"I have opened the door of my heart. I am coming tonight with my congratulations. Harry."
"STILL SAVED, Willie" (and a picture of a ship in full steam).
"With respect from a dreadful sinner aged nine."
"From the boy you asked to see Jesus, Peter."
"From your truely and loving and serious follower."

And one, almost illegible on account of the many kisses:

"I'm glad I gave my heart to God and I am tryeing and tryeing to be good. I remain your loving friend SAM SMITH SAVED."

The missions were not always conducted alone, and he learned much from his fellow-workers. He joined Bishop Taylor Smith at a T.M.C.A. rally, and worked with Mr. Archibald at Prestwick. Edmund Clark, the Rev. Jesse Mayo, Fred Glover, Frank Challis,

James Cutting and E. H. Sargent, were all associated with him in those early years, and by the end of 1906 he was beginning to be well known, and reports of his missions were beginning to appear in local papers.

"Mr. Pope is admirably adapted to this type of work and wins children by the score," commented the *Wakefield Express,* and this was certainly true. But, under the Spirit of God, his success was also due to careful, thorough preparation beforehand, and sheer hard work at the time of the mission. His usual quota was three meetings a day, and often five on Sunday. The gaps between the missions were short, but he managed to find time to write and have circulated the straightforward little 'preparatory letters' which must have disposed many a parent in his favour before ever they saw him.

To the Children & Young People

Swanley, Kent.
January, 1908.

My dear Boys and Girls,

I am coming to see you soon, all being well, and have got something simply grand to tell you. It is about Someone Who can make a grumbler cheerful, Who can turn a person who cheats at school into a straightforward person, Who can alter people's faces, and change their lives, and Who loves children very much.

So be sure to come and bring your friends with you, and we shall have a splendid time. Don't miss *one* meeting! Pray much, expect more!

With much love, hoping soon to meet you,
I am, your sincere friend,
R. Hudson Pope.

Trevanion,
Penzance.

Letter from the Missioner

My dear Children and Young People,

We are hoping soon to meet one another, are we not? and when we do meet I want you to get to know my dearest and closest Friend. He loved me and knew me long before I properly knew Him, in fact I have really only known Him for fourteen years. But more about my Friend when we meet.

Have you got a Bible? I mean, one of your *own?*; if so, whatever you do, don't forget to bring it to the meetings. Also bring your brains, your voice, and a smile, and then we are sure to have a happy time.

Then will you pray every day this prayer:

"O God, will you please save Girls and Boys during the mission, for Jesus Christ's sake. Amen."

> Your loving friend,
> R. HUDSON POPE.

13a Warwick Lane,
London, E.C.

And when the mission was over and the 'harvest' gathered in, and those eager little newborn souls handed back to the shepherd-care of their Sunday school teachers, he did not forget them, as the following letter, written after he left the district, shows.

"By the time you read this our meetings will be over, and things will be going on as usual, and yet not as usual if the real purpose of our meeting is to be understood. The purpose was that we should get to know the Lord Jesus Christ and His power to save and keep. I wonder if this is what the result of the mission has been in your life? True, we have got to know and love one another, but now the missioner is no longer here and we cannot speak to him about these things, is all to go wrong again? NO, NO, because it is not the missioner that keeps you from sin, but the Lord Jesus Christ Himself. Remember, your keeping straight lies not in your holding on to Jesus, but in His holding on to you, 'able to keep you from falling'. The best way to do it is to let Him do it for you. And if anyone says, 'How do you know you are saved?' you reply, 'Because God says so'.
Your loving Uncle Dick."

His own diaries, kept in the form of a sort of journal during those years, give glimpses of the results of those missions.

"Very cheering to find a large party of children, from a place where I had recently held a mission, attending the Annual S.U. Meetings at King's Hall, and it gave me great joy when a girl of sixteen said she felt the Lord was calling her to the mission field."

"A converted Roman Catholic boy was given a Bible, and forbidden to come to the meetings in consequence. A worker met him in the street, and the following conversation occurred:

'Why don't you write to Mr. Pope? He'd like to hear from you.'
'My mother wouldn't like me to.'
'Can't you do it without her knowing?'
'Well, yes . . . but that wouldn't be shining for Jesus, would it?'"

Yes, there was much fruit. Those hundreds and hundreds of quaint, soiled, crumpled little letters are still extant, telling of the difference that Christ had made to many a drab childhood. Those simple little testimonies seem worth preserving as the child's expression of his own individual experience of salvation. After

On Trial with the C.S.S.M.

all, what does it all mean to an eight- to twelve-year-old? Here are some of the answers:

"I am so glad I have come to Jesus, it has made me feel so much brighter. When I got to bed last night I was so happy I could not go to sleep."

"I have decided to come to Jesus and be a good boy. I want to go to heaven like Edith and Doris and George."

"Something said will you come to be a lamb of God, and I said I would and it was like as if everything had gone and it came like as if Jesus was talking to me about how He died for me. Thank you for getting me to God."

"I come to pray I will let Jesus into my heart, and grow up to leave beer alone."

"I got saved last night, Friday; Jesus brought me to His fold like a lost sheep, Oh pope, how glad my mother and father and sisters are and how glad you will be to know I have done it."

"I am not little poor Edith, I am a sinner saved by grace. Oh, I am so glad I can call myself one of Jesu's lambs. I, a poor girl, was saved in a desk. So goodbye from the girl who has come Edith."

"Last night I heard Jesus speaking to me and saying my dear little girl I have forgiven all your sins. Mary."

"Just a line to tell you know I have found the Saviour and I have cast all my sins overboard and they have sunk. Dear Mr. Pope I hope to meet you again some day and tell you all about my wicked life. Dear Mr. Pope, when I woke up this morning, I felt as fresh as a daisy and as cheery as if I'd got a gold watch."

"I was trying to make myself much better, but you said come as you are so I came."

"I was a sinner till my friends told me you was converting people, so after a few meetings I have give the Lord my sole."

And sometimes the desire is there but the step has not been taken:

"I would like to come to Jesus. I could arrange it tonight if possible."

CHAPTER SIX

Ethel Stacey and Her Spartans

So the years rolled on and mission succeeded mission; the tin trunks of letters became fuller, and the Scripture Union branches, with their attendant correspondence, became more and more extensive. And all the time that Spirit-given longing to see souls won for Christ was growing deeper, and there seem to have been few moments in his life when he was not actively on the alert, hungering for opportunities to speak of his Saviour.

Some of these incidents have been preserved for us in his old diaries. Here is one of them:

"On Friday morning I went off on my journeys again. Arrived at King's Cross about 10.15. I found my way to the 10.30 Great Northern Express for Leeds. It is a lovely train, corridor carriages, and all steam-heated, with a dining-car attached. I had prayer that God would give me a boy to speak to on the way up, but at first I did not see how that prayer was to be answered, for there was no boy in my carriage. So I made my way into the dining-car to take my seat for dinner, and sure enough opposite me at the table sat a boy of about sixteen years of age, on his way home from school. How to start the conversation was the next thing, but this the Lord arranged for me too. In the other corner of the carriage sat a clergyman, and he presently began to look round for his bag which he thought he had lost. From where I sat I could see a black bag labelled 'Jericho', under the seat. I said, 'Are you going to Jericho, sir?' 'No,' he replied, 'I'm coming back, but my bag has the old label on it.' So we pulled it out, and the old boy was as pleased as could be. My table companion and I soon fell to talking about Jericho, and got up quite a conversation, which eventually drifted on to the Licensing Bill. Said my companion, 'You will never stop drunkenness by law'. 'No,' said I, 'but you can do it by grace; a converted man will not get drunk.' Then, seizing my opportunity, I preached Christ to him. It was all new to him to hear the real Gospel, and several times I said that perhaps he had rather I did not go on, but he insisted on my finishing, so out came my Bible, and we had the whole thing from the Word. I believe the boy fully saw God's plan of salvation. . . . May I add that you will all do well to keep your eyes open for opportunities for service for the

Master. They come at very unexpected times and in funny places, but if you are in *real* touch, they *do* come, and God will open the way for a talk, even if it comes via 'Jericho' and the 'Licensing Bill'!! And never go out without a Bible, you will often need it!"

And this on his 'holiday', after a disappointing church service, when his suggestion of an open air meeting after the service had been firmly refused:

"I came out sad that I had not heard the Gospel that day proclaimed, and sad because I had been denied the privilege of speaking for the Master. However, I prayed much that somehow God would let me speak a word for Him that day, and I asked Him to give me a boy for my three-mile walk home. Sure enough, soon I spied in front three lads about fifteen, sixteen and seventeen years respectively. I hurried on and caught them up, whereupon two (the younger) went into their homes just nearby, and left me with one. He had cycled into this village from Maidstone that afternoon, his tyre had burst irreparably, and he tried to get a train, but lost it, so had to walk home! Now tell me that God had not *planned* all that! I told him I was walking the same way, and so together we went. I began at once to preach Christ to him. Found that he was relying on his baptism as a baby for his salvation, and he told me he had been confirmed a little while before, but as to what had happened then he was somewhat hazy. He owned that in spite of both his life was all wrong. How glad I was to knock away all his false foundations and help him to put his feet firmly on the Rock Christ Jesus. I gave him my card at parting and asked him to write and tell me when he had definitely yielded to Christ, and yesterday morning (June 1st) I had the joy of receiving the letter I was so longing for! Praise the Lord!! Pray for the lad—you see the only kind of teaching he gets and he will need all our prayers!"

In the same diaries we have glowing accounts of individual missions, and sometimes he visited districts two years running and had the joy of finding his children saved the previous year pressing on and growing up in Christ. The following account of his visit to Stalybridge in 1907 is probably fairly typical of many an early mission:

What! Saturday morning already! Only just time to catch the train, eh! Well, here you are, Cabby, and there'll be an extra 2d "for the horse" if we catch it. All luggage on board? Box, bike, violin-case, umbrella, lantern slides, rug, writing-case, nothing else—goodbye! "Come on, porter, label this lot for Stalybridge." That's the way! I thought the handle would be off that trunk before long, and there it goes!! That's it—at last, now we're off, and I must collect a thought or two. It is dreadful when you have to carry all your household effects about with you (specially when the handle comes off the trunk!)

Whilst we are getting to Stalybridge I will tell you a little bit about the place. It is partly in Lancashire and partly in Cheshire (the latter place, as you know, noted for its cheese and cats). It is a mill town, chiefly taken up with the cotton industry, and in a fairly flourishing condition as you will guess when I tell you that from the hillside nearby I counted eighty factory chimneys, and then I could not see all that I am told are there. I have very happy memories of a mission held here in February, 1906, and of a subsequent revisit for a weekend a month or two back. That particular part of the country seems to rejoice in a maximum of cold and a minimum of sunshine, for certainly the sun does not waste any strength there, and rain is fairly constant. I found all expectantly awaiting the mission, and on the evening of my arrival (Saturday, April 11th) we had a very nice prayer meeting specially to seek blessings on the mission. I stayed with the Rev. and Mrs. Sutcliffe (the vicar and his wife) and right hospitable people are they, and full of zeal for the work of the Lord. They have been at Stalybridge for twenty-six years and so begin to know the place!

On Sunday morning I went to Holy Trinity Church, and read the Lessons, and in the afternoon conducted the service for men only, at which about 350 were present. It was an inspiring sight to see them all. I also sang for them two selections from Handel's *Messiah*, and a piece called "The Sinner and the Song", which they had remembered from my last visit. Back to tea, and then a splendid service in the evening at the mission hall, at which I have reason to believe many turned to the Lord. It was especially pleasing to meet some of the converts of two years ago and find them shining brightly for Jesus, and some of them beginning to work for Him in Sunday school or mission hall. My own opinion is that if the labours of a pastor or of an evangelist are not producing *workers*, they are not doing very much. Paul's instruction to Timothy was—"The things that thou hast heard of me, among many witnesses, the same commit thou to faithful men, *who shall be able to teach others also*" (2 Tim. 2.2). If this does not mean "make workers", what does it mean?

I cannot stop to tell you specially and in detail all about the meetings of the mission because they were many, but we had a meeting in the day schools each day at 4.15—girls one afternoon and boys the next, and a service in the mission hall each evening at 7.00. The evening meetings were very difficult to take because of the difference in age of those coming (ranging from three to about eighty). So I used to give a short time for the small ones first, and then let them go home whilst the others would stay for a further hour to hear the Scriptures expounded. I find that people like having the Scriptures simply expounded, and will listen for hours. I took up special subjects—such as:

1. The Gospel.
2. Salvation—what from?—what for?
3. Old Nature and New Birth.
4. Resting and Working.
5. Sin.
6. Justification by Faith,

and so on throughout the week. The young people would take notes of the addresses, and the Lord drew many to Himself through His Word. After one of these meetings a young lad was staying behind, and I went to him and asked if he were "right with God". He replied "Yes," but fearing lest he should not be quite certain, I further questioned him thus: "What grounds have you for thinking you are 'right with God'?" Then came the old, old, time-worn reply which one reads of in story books and yet imagines never really is believed in by anybody—"I go to church regularly every Sunday, I read my Bible, I say my prayers, isn't that all right?" Opening my Bible at Titus 3.5, I showed him that God would only meet sinners in one way if they wanted to be saved, and that must be in *mercy*. I showed him that the things he trusted in could never save him, and dwelt on his sin, and his need of someone outside himself to save him from it. Then how glad I was to be able to point him to Christ, in Whom he found salvation, and was able to say that he would

> Cast this deadly *doing* down,
> Down at Jesus' feet:
> Stand in Him, in Him alone,
> Gloriously complete!

The next Sunday that he was able to come he had brought another lad with him who desired to know the "truth as it is in Jesus". One of the surest signs of the new life in any soul is the new desire for the salvation of others. Although the meetings were for the young people especially, yet many of the older folk gathered with us. One woman came out for Christ very definitely one evening, and then asked if we would specially pray for her husband. He came with her each evening, and was evidently under deep conviction of sin. On the last Sunday night of the mission I was called across the hall by one of the workers to speak to this very man. We talked long, and he seemed very much in earnest, and wished to be saved, but was inclined to put it off (I think because others were standing round). But by and by, the Lord won the day, and we knelt together regardless of others present, and this dear man gave himself up wholly to the Lord Jesus. He then went straight to his wife, and with tears in his eyes told her the good news, and as I watched them go down the hall arm in arm, and with their little lad of six years holding Father's hand, I blessed God for the power which saves and makes new men and women. Let infidels laugh and sceptics scoff, but ask them to produce results like this from their scepticism, and they must slink away defeated!

It seemed that I was not to get away from that hall, for someone else was waiting—a widow who wanted to say thank you for the interest taken in her son, who had been converted during the mission. I took the opportunity of asking her whether she was in a position spiritually to help the boy in his new life; but found she was not. It was a great joy to lead her gently to Christ, the help of the widow, the Father of the fatherless, and together we knelt and she found peace. Calling her son to her, I put their hands together, and thus they went home. Praise the Lord! There were still several girls waiting to see me, and it was a great joy to lead some of them into the light, and to give others a word of encouragement in the Christian life.

One evening I was talking with a party of Christian boys (converts at the two years ago mission) and the Spirit led me to speak of "unmadeup quarrels". After going on strong for a quarter of an hour, one boy said, "Well, sir; you have been hitting me hard tonight. Did you know about so and so?" mentioning two boys' names. I explained that I was not particularly hitting at anybody, although I did know something about his difficulty with the boys he mentioned. He went right out from the room and sought his two companions, and the quarrel was made up.

The fellows there have what they call a "Keenites" meeting, that is to say, those who are "keen" for the Master meet once a week in one of their own houses and read the Scripture Union portion and have prayer. I had the joy of speaking at one of these meetings. The parlour was cheerful and bright, and packed with boys in every available corner, and wasn't it hot! One boy led the meeting, another read, and another led in prayer, and I spoke. Then we had a prayer meeting, and it was goodly to hear those mill lads pour out their simple petitions to God and thank Him for His power. Upon my word, it put some of our respectable church prayer meetings to shame, where experienced Christians find it hard to utter even a word or two in prayer. Oh, for Christ's sake, for the love of suffering, sinning humanity, for the boys and girls struggling with temptation and needing our prayers every day—PRAY, PRAY, and *PRAY TONIGHT*! Pray for these very boys; they are laughed at in their mills every day because they belong to Christ and serve Him; they have, some of them, no help at home; they are longing and reaching forth to a higher knowledge of Christ and His love, and the persecution is nearly as great for many of these boys as for a heathen who turns to the Christian religion.

Yet although the outward pattern of these years was much the same, and mission followed mission, to the young man himself they were eventful in the extreme. In the spring of 1907 he went to conduct a series of meetings in Leeds, and he stayed with Dr. and Mrs. Stacey, a devoted Christian couple who kept open house for all the Lord's servants. R. H. P. conducted this mission with his usual zest, but actually he was far more interested in the mission that was already going on in Dr. Stacey's home, run by their daughter Miss Ethel Stacey, who seemed to have had a real gift for handling boys.

Her group of lads, which numbered sixty to seventy, called themselves the Spartans, and they met in a large attic for games on week-nights, and for a Bible class on Sundays. They had a Spartan membership card, a printed declaration of their faith in Christ, and their resolution to serve Him. Its direct outspokenness, which allowed for no compromise, appealed to R. H. P., as did its authoress:

> I believe the whole Bible to be the inspired Word of God.
> I believe the doctrine of atonement by the blood of Jesus Christ.
> I believe that Christ died for my sins and rose again according to the Scriptures.
> I believe Jesus Christ to be the divine Son of God.
> I also intend by the help of God to live a true, consistent Christian life, to refrain from those habits which may become a snare and a danger to my fellow-Spartans:
> 1. Smoking.
> 2. Attendance at theatres, music halls, balls, dances.
> 3. Playing billiards and any card games specially associated with gambling.
> 4. Taking any strong drink as a beverage.

He addressed the group on several occasions, and their mutual love for the Lord and for boys quickly developed into a deep love for each other. His visits to Leeds became more and more frequent, and one day in 1908 he took her up into her Spartan attic and asked her to marry him.

It must have been a great decision for the quiet, rather timorous girl. She had been brought up in a wealthy home, waited on by servants, her favourite hobby riding. Now she faced marrying a young man who earned £150 a year, who would seldom be at home, and who, even as he declared his love, impressed on her that the Lord's work must always come first. It was small wonder that she hesitated. "Couldn't you do some work that would keep you nearer home, Dick?" she asked wistfully. The answer was a final and irrevocable "No".

So Ethel made her choice, and they were married at Woodhouse

Lane Methodist Church in Leeds in 1910. They set up house together at Shadwell, Leeds. As envisaged, he was very seldom at home, and she kept loyally to her part of the bargain. Sometimes, when she was in poor health, she had to send for him, but she never detained him long, and when the question arose as to whether it was his duty to stay with her, she would remind him gently, "Don't you remember what you promised, Dick?"

To casual onlookers her help may have seemed of a negative kind, for she was a retiring personality. She did not travel with him, or take much part in meetings, although she joined him as house-mother at his beach missions in July and August, and wrote a few booklets. But she stayed at home, willingly accepting the loneliness that such a life involved, quietly economizing and denying herself so that he might have his full freedom; and by her very presence supplying the background of peace and human love that he so sorely needed in his exhausting life of travel and change. He saw comparatively little of her, but he idealized her, and the very thought of her was an inspiration to him; she was always there, constant, quiet, upholding him in prayer, and on her he could pour out all the passionate tenderness of his rather shy nature. Spiritually they were one, and their home was a happy one. Speaking of her in November 1960, on the occasion of his retirement, he said,

> "She had adaptability, stickability, musical ability and the ability and willingness to shoulder the burdens which fall to the lot of an evangelist's wife. But for her unselfishness, self-denial and co-operation, much of the work which I have, by God's grace, been able to accomplish, would have been impossible. I think she has held a record ... for she spent every August without a break for fifty-three years as a helper in a seaside mission—first with Mr. Hutcheson, then with Mr. Edmund Clark, and latterly with me."

In 1911 their only child, John, was born, and what that birth must have meant to that ardent lover of children can only be imagined. Alone, he climbed Baildon Heights, and looking down on a sun-drenched world he wrote the following lines:

> God's boy—our boy! Yes, His and ours together
> Given to God before his little frame
> Wrought by joint love of father and of mother
> Into this world of light and shadow came,
> Given by God to us—and given back.
>
> Our Jack.

> God's boy—our boy! God give us needed wisdom
> Rightly to lead the little life He gave
> Till, in the days to come he may lead others
> And in his turn be used to help and save;
> God's boy for aye, now and when childhood's gone.
> Our John.

The tremendous sense of responsibility that weighed on him as he entered into fatherhood is best described in his own words, about fifty years later:

> "Forty-nine years ago a little child came to us, and God has used that little child, no longer little, to be another part of the secret of a life yielded to the Lord. It was not merely a case of going to other people's children, but it was someone that belonged to me myself. I pray God one day you may have that joy. But it is a terrific responsibility. How shall I tell the little one? I myself must be all God wants me to be. And again here is the necessity for the disciplined life, because of someone else watching us; someone else always watching. How shall I tell him? He is very, very small; he is in his cradle. He won't understand anything you say to him. Very well, we are going to say it, nevertheless! The Holy Spirit must have something to work on. When he is going to sleep, his father and mother will sing to him. "Poor boy," you say. Would you like to know what I sang? A lot of beautiful things like hey diddle diddle? Not when he was going to sleep. I will tell you what we sang. "Jesus, Thy blood and righteousness, my beauty are, my glorious dress", and out of old *Golden Bells*, "Jesus was the first to love us ... Now our sins may all be covered by the precious blood He shed"—the precious blood, to the baby in the cradle? another life to whom to set an example, another one to bring up questions which must be answered."

It was not easy to bring up a child of whom he saw so little, and the training was probably a well-tempered mixture of tenderness and sternness. But when he was at home he spent every possible moment with his boy, cycling, walking, swimming, making a railroad all over the garden with a complicated signal system; then he was off again to all those hundreds of other children, each one more precious to him than ever, because of the little boy he left at home.

1914—the opening months of the war, and a period of keen conflict to R. H. P. He felt that the truest patriotism was to carry on his work, and prepare the children for the storm ahead. He registered as a minister of religion, but suffered agonies of apprehension when called before the tribunal. But God was overruling that trial, for there was a Christian man of authority present who pleaded his cause. "I should like to state the extreme value of his work," he said, "especially now, in the absence of parental discipline." He won his case, and was set free to carry on. And carry on he did, all through those dark years, travelling on troop trains, preaching in dimly-lighted halls, preaching in air-raid shelters, preaching while bombs fell. But the harvests were rich. Fathers and older brothers were out at the front, and many a little child had known the shadow of death in its home, or carried its share of the family's anxiety. Never had the refuge been more needed; never had the open door of heaven seemed brighter. Many an anxious little heart found peace, and might have echoed the sentiments of the following letter:

> "To a good friend who is trying to learn me as much as he can about my Crist in heaven above. I want to be a cristian till my death and when death comes he will call me and I will answer him with a light heart and say 'I will come'."

CHAPTER SEVEN

Secrets of Success

"SOULS were won all the way along . . . I saw it steadily all the time . . . many, many came . . ." he mused when nearing the end of the journey, and a friend who yearned to see blessing begged him to reveal his secret. "Did you ever consciously have some tremendous experience of the filling of the Holy Spirit, or some mighty anointing of God for this work?"

"No; I just kept in touch all the time. I often came to a meeting with no preconceived plan. I always used Bible words freely, and told the child the Bible truths on which he was to act even if, at first, he could not understand them. The Spirit works on the Word, and time and the Spirit explain."

"But what about their problems and questions?"

"You can't explain anything to a dead child. But by preaching the Word you are giving the Spirit something to work on. When the child is saved and the work of the Spirit goes on in a living heart, the questions mostly fall away. You must await God's time."

"But to be so sure of God's time and leading . . . to be so dependent on God . . . how did you learn to know God in such a way?"

"I learned to know God as I worked for Him. I never had much time to be introspective. Some say 'How easy it would be to serve Him if we could only see Him'; He tells us we should see Him if we would only serve Him."

"Have you known what it is to agonize in prayer? to spend nights wrestling for souls?"

"No, I have never known wrestling, agonizing prayer. When I've told the Lord about it, I usually go to sleep. You must remember that I work among children, and one tends to identify oneself with those among whom one works. The prodigal struggled back to the father's house from the far country, but the child has not yet strayed so far. The soldier, conscious of hostile, adverse forces, fears and wrestles; the child, conscious of those same forces, fears and creeps into its father's arms."

"Besides, the work was so exacting, I was always too tired to spend nights in prayer; I needed my sleep. I prayed before my missions, and worked during my missions. Once the mission started it was just a short quiet time before breakfast, and then a keeping in touch, moment by moment, all through the business of the day."

"Do you put a great deal of preparation into your talks?"

"A tremendous lot of thought and care went into the preparation of my models—hours of thought as to the simplest way to present such truths as grace, regeneration, faith, substitution, redemption, etc. But once made, I have used the model and the same address hundreds of times over. That does not mean that one need not prepare again. You may safely use the address a hundred times, as long as you pray about it as much the hundredth time as you did the first time. When I've preached a sermon twenty times I just begin to understand it myself. I have never set aside a great deal of time for preparation. I learned to use the spare moments—the pacing up and down on platforms, the railway journeys, the walks to and fro to the meetings. But whatever sermon I decide to preach, there are always two questions of paramount importance which I keep resolutely before myself:

1. What do I want them to know that they did not know before?
2. What do I want them to do that they have never done before?"

"You must realize", he wrote to one of his critics, "that each child is a sinner needing a Saviour. Here many addresses to children fall short. They are often stories with a moral, showing the need for a child to be thoughtful and kind and good. Some speakers add that these things cannot be done without the help of the Lord Jesus; others point to Him as the example; but unless you are speaking to converted children, this is only another way of teaching salvation by works. Of course, there is a time and place for instruction in Christian conduct, and doctrine and practice should always intertwine, but it is the doctrine that is so often missing from our talks to children, and unless the matters of sin and guilt are dealt with, it is not much use to present the Lord Jesus as Saviour.

"In Matthew 18 [which Mr. Pope called 'the children's charter], the Lord tells us some very important things about children:

v. 10   they are very precious,
v. 11   they are lost,

v. 12   they are gone astray,
v. 14   they are perishing,
v. 6   they can be stumbled by older people, or they can believe in Jesus.

"Some lovers of children find it hard to believe these statements, for children are such jolly little people, and in some we see little evidence of sin. This is because we only see the out-working, and in many children not much has, as yet, out-worked. But there is the evil heart within, only waiting to proceed, and until the grace of God intervenes, the child has a sinful heart and will pursue a sinful course."

He did not frighten them with much talk of eternal punishment or hell, although in one of his models he showed a bridge over to Glory-Land from Sin-Land and Shame-Land and Sorrow-Land, but no bridge over from Satan-Land, and he pleaded very solemnly and earnestly for the children to cross over in time. But mostly, he just spoke of sin; what it does to the sinner himself, what effect it has on others, and what it did to the Lord Jesus, and as he spoke he believed that the Holy Spirit was working in him, and as a result thousands of children were shown their deep need of Jesus.

The very best children were never left in doubt that *all* had sinned, and he loved to tell the story of how he once arrived early at a mission hall where he was due to preach. A small girl also arrived early, and, her shyness having been dispelled by the friendly stranger, she pointed up to a text on the wall and remarked, "I can tell you the answer to that one, because there aren't any".

R. H. P. looked at the text and read, "Jesus Christ came into the world to save sinners".

"I don't understand," he said. "It isn't a question, so how can it have an answer?"

"Well, sir," she replied, "the gent who spoke last night taught us that text, and then he asked us, 'Why didn't Jesus come into the world to save good people?' and please, sir, I can tell you the answer, because there aren't any."

But no child was ever left in darkness of self-despair. With a sure hand they were led through and on to the Cross and the Saviour.

"It is here", wrote R. H. P., "that you must tell the story of the Cross, and preach Christ crucified, as Paul did. I try to introduce this story, fairly fully told, into every address, and there is nothing like it for bringing a hush over the audience. Begin with the last supper, the garden of Gethsemane, the scourging, the procession to Calvary, the mocking crowds, and God laying our sins on Jesus in the dark ... the work finished, the life handed back to God; everything done that needed to be done that children might be saved from sin and sinning. Then you must tell how God raised Him from the dead, and how He is alive now and able to save to the uttermost. Some have hesitated to tell the story of the Cross to young children, but you need not fear to do this, provided you use the restrained language of Scripture.

"Paint the background of your Gospel picture as dark as you like, as long as, in the foreground you put the glorious figure of the Lord Jesus Christ Whose beauty and light will sparkle against the background."

Childhood is the age of extremes. Sorrows are never perhaps so black and hopeless again, but once the burden is lifted it is soon forgotten, and the contrasting joy and relief will never again be so golden. Out of the darkness of conviction he led them, into the light of forgiveness and peace with God. Lingering over some of these testimonies one seems to sense the very joy of heaven. One can imagine them dancing home, on feet so light that they would scarcely touch the paving stones.

"I feel as though tons and tons of lead had been lifted from my heart."

"I decided for Christ on January 28th. I feel as though a fountain of water were placed to refresh me. I feel as happy as the day is long."

"I have done it, and it has made me more happy than I have been in all my life before. Before I came to Jesus my heart was full of sin, but now it is not because Jesus has carried it away on His back."

He expected decisions and he got them, all the way along. If no decisions were registered a strange lowness of spirit assailed him; he became silent, troubled, preoccupied until, as he put it, 'the break came', and the trunks of letters show practically no mission without its harvest of visible results. How lasting these decisions have proved to be will be discussed later on.

He expected and appealed to the child to come to Christ, to open his heart, to cross the bridge, to enter the door, to put his name in the envelope, or to act on whatever simile he happened to have used. Yet the time and method of these appeals were quite unpredictable, and in no part of his work was he more conscious of the guidance of the Holy Spirit. Sometimes no appeal would be made at all. "I didn't feel it was the moment to pull in the net," he would explain, or "I didn't feel I ought to press for decision". On other occasions it was just the opposite. "The Lord let me loose on them," he would say exultingly, and dozens would indicate their desire to be saved, and flock to his after-meeting.

Very quiet and holy were some of these after-meetings, when each child was spoken to and prayed with personally. Yet no high-pressure or persuasive tactics were used. Usually, the ice was broken by a quiet talk about the child itself, its name and age, and then, the conversation was steered gently round to the reason why the child had stayed behind. Although he relied on the Spirit to guide the conversation, he had his own rules of technique which he was ready to pass on to younger workers.

"Will you tell me why you have stayed tonight? Have you already given your heart to Jesus, or do you want to?" If you find that the child had settled the matter in the meeting, do not urge a second settlement. Go on to speak about being sure, and point out such texts as John 6.37; John 1.12, 13; 1 John 2.12, stressing "for His Name's sake". Pray with the child, a prayer of thanks to God, and get him to pray for himself also. Then jot down on a piece of paper the verses you have shown him, and tell him to underline them in his Bible before he goes to bed.

If, however, the child has stayed because he wants to be saved, ask some questions to find out how much he has understood, and in what special way the Holy Spirit is leading his thinking. Point out suitable texts to meet his particular need, and then suggest that he then and there receives Jesus, or trusts Him, or opens his heart to Him, or asks Him to come in, or whatever has been the line of the message. It is always well to follow the thought that has been stressed by the speaker, rather than going off in some other direction and perhaps confusing the mind of the child. That is to say, if the message has been about letting the Lord Jesus into the heart, follow that line and do not speak about 'coming to Jesus' or some other line of thought. If the idea has been 'coming to Jesus', here are some texts to use. Why must I come? Isaiah 1.18, because my sins are as scarlet and crimson—scarlet, the colour that stands out most and comes out least. Am I invited? Yes, Matthew 11.28, "Come unto Me", Jesus said. Will He receive me if I do come? Yes, John 6.37, "him that cometh to Me I will in no wise cast out". And WHEN should I come? Isaiah 1.18, "Come now". How should I come? Mark 2.17, just as I am, for Jesus said, "I came not to call the righteous, but sinners".

If you find the child does not seem to have understood, try to ascertain what the difficulty is and clear it up with your Bible. It is a good thing not only to point to certain texts, but to get him to read them aloud to you.

If you are ever led to ask a child such a question as "Are you saved?" or "Are you a Christian?" or "Have you accepted Christ?" be sure you always give an alternative, such as "Are you a Christian, or haven't you got as far as that yet?" or "Have you accepted the Saviour, or are you just thinking about the matter?" or, "I gather you want to be a real Christian, but you do not quite understand what it means yet and would like me to help you". If you do not give the alternative, the child is put into the difficult position of having to say "Yes" or "No", and may say yes when it has not got as far as that, but thinks yes is what it ought to say. You yourself will also then be in a difficult position as to how to proceed with the talk.

Sometimes a word of personal testimony will help, but do not make that too prominent, lest your hearer should think she must have an experience like yours before she can be saved.

Do not exert undue pressure. One reason for spurious conversions is putting pressure on a child beyond the point to which the Holy Spirit has led him. If you ask, how can you know the way in which the Holy Spirit is leading, the reply is, only by being yourself so in touch with the Spirit, and so filled with Him, that He Who is working in both yourself and the child may Himself be your Guide.

And with all who came he was very gentle, nor did he worry over much if there were sometimes bursts of nervous giggling. "It may be an emotional reaction," he would say, "do *not* take it for granted that nothing has happened or that the child is not in earnest." Sometimes he would be told that a child had professed conversion at an earlier date, and this did not worry him either. "A little boy needs a little boy's Saviour, and a bigger boy needs a bigger boy's Saviour," he once said, and while quietly seeking to lead the child back to the memory of that first transaction, he would recognize his desire for further light. When children came to the after-meeting two nights running, he would ask them to tell the others in the group what happened on the previous evening. He loved to remind his young workers of cripple Maisie, aged eleven, who returned to the little back room the evening following her conversion.

"But, Maisie," said her teacher, "didn't you come to Jesus last night?"

"Oh, yes," replied Maisie, "it's not me now, it's my friend."

But it was not always he who conducted those after-meetings. Sometimes he was not needed.

"I was speaking in a church," he once said, "and I told the children they could come back if they wanted to, and I would be there. Then the vicar brought some visitors in and accidentally shut the door on two little girls, Mary and Alice, aged seven, who were just coming in because they wanted to come to the Saviour." It was a cold winter's night, but Alice told him later what they did. "I said to Mary, let's do it on the step; it will be just as good. So we knelt down on the step and gave our hearts to Jesus, and it *was* just as good, wasn't it, Mr. Pope?" There was no need for the man in church. They did it on the step, and it was just as good.

"Tell me wherein thy great strength lieth." First and foremost in his constant communion with Christ and his complete dependence on the Holy Spirit. The practical outworking of this dependence might be condensed into eight factors:

1. He loved the children with a natural and a spiritual love.
2. He spoke with authority and simplicity.
3. He spoke of sin that they might be convicted.
4. He spoke of the cross that they might be saved.
5. He expected decisions—and got them.
6. He expected moral results—and saw them.
7. He taught them to be soul-winners.
8. He committed them back to the care of their local churches, or followed them up himself.

CHAPTER EIGHT

Did the Converts Last?

MANY criticisms of R. H. P.'s methods have been raised. Is it not dangerous to ask children to act when their emotions are stirred, and others are pressing forward? How many of these decisions, made in the warmth and glow and excitement of the mission hall, under the influence of an exceedingly attractive personality, really lasted?

It is impossible to give any calculated answer to these questions. The vast majority of the Lizzies and Ivys and Tommys and Georges of the 1920s are scattered and gone, and there is no way of tracing whether they grew to love and serve God, or not. No fine building ever rose without corresponding heaps of waste and rubble. But one thing is certain. A very large number have stood firm, and many of these are now prominent disciples. Over and over again R. H. P.'s heart was cheered by a letter from a grown man or woman in active service for God who looks back gratefully to the day when, in the lighted mission hall or church, or in the quite of the after-meeting, or crosslegged on the beach, they came to Christ as a result of Mr. Pope's messages.

> "If your memory can go back twenty-two years ago, you may remember I was one of the converts at a mission you conducted in Bristol . . . Last year I was made a deacon of the Baptist chapel, and superintendent of the Sunday school . . . however imperfectly, I am still following Him."
>
> "I remember when, as a lad of ten, you set me on the upward path at the tent mission at Brockham Green twenty-three years ago . . . after all that time I am still serving the same Jesus as you showed me."
>
> "Thirty-six years ago you took a mission for us at Wilmington, and three lads came up to the house after you came home one evening, and you led them to the Lord. One I have lost sight of, but Arthur has recently been to preach at our mission. The third 'boy' is now a harbour master, and he tells me that what he learned that night has been his sheet anchor all his life."

"I was asked by our pastor to write concerning the results of the mission held by you here some years ago. Last night Miss H. came before the church and gave her testimony. She is the fourth to be baptized and received into fellowship as a direct result of that mission."

"I felt I would like to write to you on the eve of sailing as a missionary to China.... In December 1935 you conducted a mission in Bolton, and it was at one of those meetings that I came to know my Saviour. Since then He has become more and more precious to me, so much so that I feel I must go and tell others."

There are photographs, signed on the back:

"With all kind regards and thanks for introducing me to the Good Shepherd on 18.7.23. I went out as a medical missionary exactly sixteen years later."

"I was thirteen years old when you came to our school and told me to put my little link into His strong link. Thank God the link has held."

These letters and testimonies could be multiplied indefinitely, and R. H. P. exulted in news of his 'little children' who had grown on into men of God. He answered them all, checking the dates, for every child who ever professed conversion was carefully recorded.

"I was simply delighted to open your letters this morning," he wrote to two brothers in 1960. "I do think it was jolly of you to have written. I straightway went to my record book, and found Southwold 1930—J. H., aged seven; C. H., aged eight. But there was no note of what happened that Sunday evening. Evidently you did not tell me at the time."

There is an interesting list extant of the names of schoolboys who attended a mission in Edinburgh in 1923. It was perhaps the smallest mission he ever conducted, for only twenty names and addresses are recorded for the whole fortnight. Was it worth it, he may have wondered at the time.

But the results of that mission have reached out to the ends of the earth. Forty years later many of those twenty names are still traceable:

Ralph Erskine Scott, Terence Adenbrooke, and H. C. Duncan went as missionaries to India.

Scott Martin went as a missionary to Manchuria, and J. N. D. to Kenya.

George Duncan, David Lead and Gordon Kerr entered the ministry.

J. E. Duncan became C.S.S.M. Secretary for Scotland.

Mr. Pope himself would never have claimed that all professed conversions were either real or lasting. "You must allow for at least three factors in every child's profession," he once wrote, "misunderstanding, the desire to please, and the excitement of writing a letter." He himself spent much time in seeking out the causes of what he called 'spurious conversions'. The result of these reflections were published in a pamphlet entitled *True Conversion*. This has since been reprinted as part of a booklet called *Know How to Evangelize Children* which every children's evangelist would do well to read. Mr. Pope maintains that a number of these professions that bear no fruit are probably inevitable, but he lists the following contributing factors:

1. Lack of conviction of sin, resulting in a poor appreciation of the work of Christ. Little forgiveness means little love.
2. Failure to count the cost, or to impress upon the child the true meaning of the step he proposes to take.
3. Hurry on the part of the leader, largely due to insufficient stress being laid, in the mind of the worker, on that side of truth known as the sovereign, electing grace of God. No one whom God has purposed to save will be lost, and there is therefore no need for hurry, or frantic appeals, or undue pressure. If the Lord begins a work, He will finish it. If He does not begin it, no one else will.
4. The child's failure to understand, or interpret correctly, what has been said.
5. Unwise methods of drawing in the net. Signing decision cards, holding up your hand, etc., have their uses, but their danger lies in the transference of the emphasis from the heart transaction with God to the performing of a suggested act. In order to avoid this danger I like to make any such signs not simultaneously with, but subsequent to, the act of faith.
6. Levity of atmosphere or demeanour on the part of the worker.
7. The intrusion of the worker between God and the child. The measure in which a man or woman is out to attract a child to himself or herself is the measure in which he or she fails to attract that child to Christ.

8. Wrong motives. A decision to do right may not mean the coming of a convicted sinner to a crucified, risen Saviour, which is the only ground of true conversion.

In his own ministry he sought to avoid these pitfalls. He preached a 'whole Gospel'; he was never in a hurry, and the dullest child could not fail to understand the truths he taught and explained. He was often humorous, but he learned to curb himself, and his listeners were always made conscious of the reality of sin and salvation. Although his unusually attractive personality drew children irresistibly to him, he sought, as years went by, to become more and more a signpost pointing to Christ.

He himself, in his old age, marvelled in simple, grateful humility at the great number of Christian men and women who had first decided for Christ through his ministry. He attributed this partly to two positive factors, as well as to the avoidance of mistakes.

Firstly, he worked carefully and methodically with the local Sunday schools and Christian school teachers. He made detailed lists of the different classes and denominations to which the children belonged, and each one who professed conversion was given back to the special pastoral care of some older Christian. "I don't doubt the reality of their conversion," he would say, "but the result will depend on how they are fed. You might as well throw a new baby into a cabbage field and expect it to eat, as expect a babe in Christ to grow strong without proper spiritual feeding and care." His correspondence with Sunday school teachers and class leaders was heavy and varied.

Secondly, he taught his children that salvation meant not only safety, but newness of life. In fact, he usually mentioned them in the same breath. Salvation was never an end in itself, but the birth of a new child, and probably each converted child left him with a sense of expectation that life was going to be different. And in spite of the falls and disappointments, many letters testify that life was different:

> "This morning I done the hearth and the washing up, but the strangest thing of all was I did not pull a long face neither did I look miserable. Oh, the happy little meeting after the usual time!"
>
> "I am doing my best to be a real Christian. I took pity on a stray dog and took it into our house and fed it. My father says it is part of a sheep dog."

"I am trying my very utmost . . . I am trying to be a good and faithful sinner."

"The seaside mission has done much for me. In the first place it has made me much more agreeable."

Even the smallest realized that there must be a change. The following extracts are from letters written in very young handwriting indeed:

"I really have come to Jesus. I do feel so much better, and I'm knitting a scarf for the soldiers."

"I was well pleased when I came to God. Some of my playmates have seen that I have been better."

"When you spoke about slamming doors it touched my heart and at home I was very careful to shut doors quitely."

"I have turned a Christian but it is hard to keep from sinning. I was saved but I sinned from a little beleaver."

"I always annoyed my Sunday school teacher but now I will give her a surprise. If she says what has happened I will say Mr. Pope converted me from a sinner to a Christian."

"I have been saved by grace. I promise I will not give up cheek to my granny, but I will go for my granny messages."

Mr. Pope himself organized the 'Show-it-at-Home Club', and had cards printed with lists of jobs to be done. He stressed repeatedly that *it must show*.

"I'm sorry you are going," said a boy of eleven at the end of a mission, "but I've given my heart to the Lord Jesus."

"I'm very glad," replied R. H. P. "Does anyone know at home?"

"My mother does," said the boy thoughtfully. "And I think the cat knows too."

He did his best to prepare them for the temptations and disappointments ahead. How earnestly and painstakingly he would reply to the lad who wrote: "I've become a Christian, but it hasn't done me much good."

And how he loved to tell of the small boy who went home professing conversion, but whose subsequent behaviour made his mother remark that she saw little difference.

"Well, Mummy," replied her little son earnestly, "it's all of grace. It takes a long time."

Thirdly, he taught them to serve. In his often-used model, Salvation-Land led straight into Service-Land, and those converted children went home with a sense of responsibility and a

Did the Converts Last?

desire to lead someone else to the Lord. The results were sometimes startling!

> "Now, Mr. Pope, I am going to tell you the best news of all. My mother is saved, isn't it lovely? She is a different mother altogether. Now I have got to work hard to get father, and I can tell you it takes a lot of doing."
> "I am going to try and anchor my sister to Jesus. I think girls need saving just as much as boys."
> "I am going to be good for ever if I can and I am going to entice my father and mother to come tonight as well as me."
> "Tom and myself are hoping to bring at least ten people to Jesus."

One reads letters from children in Barrowbridge who were a little 'church' in a wash-house and met daily to pray for the man who had led them to Christ. There were two newly converted lads also who formed a class of boys and girls. "They wish to know more about the Lord Jesus," wrote these two young evangelists, "and we need you to give us some assistance. If you could supply us with at least half a dozen of those little books we should be most obliged."

Kindled to serve, fired by the joy of new adventure in Christ's service, those who had been truly born again did not often go back. And still the letters came in from men and women now growing old, but still pressing on.

And just occasionally he saw the work crowned and completed, and had the joy of knowing that the child whose feet he had set on the road to heaven had arrived safely. Two letters written on cheap faded notepaper tell of such triumphs.

> "You have passed on the Word to me, I intend to bring others to God. My first victim is my pal at school."
> "You will be very sorry to learn that my sister Nellie passed away this afternoon after a short and painful illness. During her delirium she said "It is glory', and sang
>   'There is a Saviour, a beautiful Saviour,
>   And He is waiting for me.' "
> "I shall never forget the addresses you gave in the Y.M.C.A. Our little girl Gladys gave her heart to Jesus that night, and was called Home to be with Him twelve months later. It makes all the difference when Jesus takes full possession of a child's soul . . . she longed to live because she wanted to go to China, and tell the Chinese children about Jesus and His love . . . oh, the joy and happy memories when we think of the times spent together over God's Word, and singing those little C.S.S.M. choruses."

So they outstripped him, and came to Zion 'with songs and everlasting joy'—a joy he now shares. As one little girl expressed it in a letter overflowing with gratitude:

> "If I get to heaven before you do I will wait for you at the gate, and when you come I will take your hand and lead you to God and say, 'This is the man who made me a Christian!'."

CHAPTER NINE

Sand and Sunshine by the Sea

So the years rolled on, and the biographer seeks in vain for chronological landmarks. There was a brief visit to Palestine and Egypt in 1934, and a few short holidays, but otherwise mission succeeded mission with almost unbroken regularity until 1944, when his wife's health made it necessary for him to spend longer periods at home. At the start of the Second World War he carried on steadily, although meetings which began in churches often ended in cellars and air-raid shelters. Beach missions were cancelled owing to the shortage of young workers and the threat of invasion, but at Ballyholme, Bangor, in Ireland, where Mr. Pope had taken over the C.S.S.M. in 1932 from the Rev. Bryan Green, the local Christians continued as usual.

"What were the highlights of those years?" he was once asked.

"There is no higher light than the salvation of a child," he replied. "That is lighted at every mission."

"I wonder if some people hold back from giving their whole life to service among children," he once said, "because there are no prospects? What *are* the prospects? After ten years you will still be a children's evangelist. After twenty years, still a children's evangelist. After forty years, still a children's evangelist. There *is* no future, not down here on earth. But what about that day when the gates of heaven are thrown wide and you march in, and all your children with you?"

But of all his children's missions perhaps those he loved best were the Children's Special Service Missions held on the beaches which he led year after year on into old age. Starting as a young worker at Llanfairfechan, he later led missions at Ilfracombe, Penmaenmawr, Southwold, Sheringham, Filey, Criccieth and Ballyholme, and these seasides seemed the perfect setting for his personality and gifts. Here, he could play with his children as well as work for them, running races right on to the end, until the day when a small child was heard enquiring, "Who is that funny old gentleman running along at the back?" Here on the beach he could give full rein to his liking for puns and jokes, which in that happy atmosphere of sand and sunshine were always uproariously successful.

"I hope you will always have dogged determination, children," he remarked from the sand pulpit when a dog insisted, despite the efforts of the workers, on standing throughout the choruses with its head resting on the organist's knee.

"Tide-fighting for the under 12s," he would announce, "but you 13-year-olds, don't think it's infra-dig to join in; you're only in-for-a-dig!"

Mr. Sharpe was expected for an evening and hadn't arrived. R. H. P. strolled in.

"You didn't see Bob Sharpe on the road, did you?" enquired an anxious worker.

"No," said R. H. P., "but I saw two notices. One said 'Bear left for Lowestoft' and the next said 'Sharp left for Lowestoft'. They may have met."

And Ballyholme birthday would hardly have been Ballyholme birthday had not R. H. P. informed them solemnly year by year that there was only one misfortune on this happy day—the cake was in tiers!

The memories came crowding over him as he looked back on fifty-six years of summer C.S.S.M.s; memories of blue seas and yellow sands, of grey days and dim parish halls; of hours crowded to the full from dawn to midnight, of Penmaenmawr in 1912. "A famous watering place where it rained nearly every day." "That was the year of the famous Scripture Union thermometer, one side 'Girling' and the other side 'Boyling' "; of a tiny tots' tea-party followed by a boys' party, and the tiny tots ate half the boys' tea as well as their own, by mistake; of a toy service, and six happy evenings spent round R. H. P.'s model of the tabernacle; of a certain Sunday afternoon when, to a hushed young audience, he spoke of the Hands of the Lord Jesus.

Criccieth in 1915; the incomparable beauty of the mountains across the bay, and the war ravaging the world outside. "Those of you who get up early", wrote R. H. P., "will know that some of the finest summer days begin with mist, and that was what happened at Criccieth. There was a great mist of difficulty and discouragement before the sunshine broke through and the day became one of the most beautiful we have ever known"—the first week, when a special well-known speaker was asked to address the girls, and only two turned up; three to the boys' meeting; eleven on the sand. But the numbers mounted steadily, until forty-two girls were being packed into a room twelve feet square, and children accepted Christ every day.

There is the memory of a boy on the Criccieth green who wanted assurance that the Lord had saved him. How could he know for certain that Jesus Christ was there? R. H. P. sought to explain, and a bright face was suddenly lifted to his. "I see it now, sir," he said, "I receive Him into my heart and reckon on Him being there whenever I want Him." A week later the face was just as bright. "I've proved it," he said, "He's always there."

"In my desk at home," says Mr. Pope, "there is a little flat stone, and on it is written 'Criccieth 1915'. I don't know how many more little stones there are like that. But at the last beach service, as we sang with bowed heads,
> In full and glad surrender
> I give myself to Thee,

everyone who really meant it was asked to pick up a little flat stone, and when they got home they were to write the date on it, as I have done with mine. I do not know how many there are, but I trust time will show very many lives consecrated to God that day."

Criccieth 1947–49. 'A mother of five' has written out her memories and impressions:

"Five children, whose ages ranged between eleven years and sixteen months, were privileged to meet the man who has been to them a staunch friend through life, for R. H. P., who seemed at first like some wonderful 'fairy godfather', soon began to weave a kind of pattern into their young lives . . . I, their mother, will never forget the countless little slips of paper pushed under the front door each evening inviting one or another to some feast or treasure hunt to be held the following day; nor the scramble of little feet in the morning, and the shrill, excited voices, 'Oh, look at this one for me . . . and one for you too, Gillian . . . and mine is a late one!' Something was arranged for every age, and even the tiny tots had their tea-parties and special lantern talks. And will those tinies ever forget the first time they learned his 'just new' tune to:
> Jesus, when He left the sky,
> And for sinners came to die,
> In His mercy passed not by
> Little ones like me.

"He was never too busy or preoccupied to give unhurried time to a puzzled little fellow of nine who wanted *really* to know just how he could ask Jesus into his life . . . and would He really stay and not go away again? How many of that age-group crowded into the kingdom during that August holiday! Sports day, tide-fights, sand-modelling, Bible object services, Pilgrim's Progress coloured slides, sausage-sizzles, were the order of the day, and through them all, in a quiet, spiritual way, our children were drawn to the children's Saviour through the loving, dedicated personality of this man of God. Small wonder that during those years our boys of seven and eleven years old accepted Christ and dedicated their lives to His service. Nor is it strange that both have now taught, at Ballyholme and Criccieth, the same wonderful truths to other children, who sit, just as they sat years ago, playing with the pebbles, but listening hard."

Elie in 1919, some nine months after Armistice. Peace was declared, but a tremendous sense of bereavement lay heavy on the land. The King had requested that July 6th should be set aside as a special thanksgiving for peace, and the C.S.S.M. gladly complied. Mr. Pope drew up bills to be given away, and 750 people gathered. Four hundred and nineteen children were presented with a Union Jack and a card attached, having on one side, 'Let the peace of God rule in your hearts', and on the other, 'Children's Special Thanksgiving for Peace. July 6th, 1919.'

The 'What I found on the Beach' service certainly tested the leader's ingenuity to the full. What are you to say when presented with a great piece of an iron bedstead, and half an onion? R. H. P., as usual, was not at a loss:

"Og, king of Bashan, was remembered by his iron bedstead . . . take care that when you are dead and gone you are not only remembered by what you went to sleep on!"

"Have you seen the tears in Mother's eyes when she peels an onion? Children, don't be like this onion. Never do anything that would bring tears to Mother's eyes."

It was at Elie that the tide did not suit the hour of the birthday service, and it was difficult to build a pulpit on stones and pebbles; some sand had to be carried, and wet sand is heavy, nor was the tide far enough down to dig until 11 p.m. But once again, R. H. P. was invincible, and he and his helpers worked in the dark with wheelbarrows, boxes and spades to erect a magnificent pulpit five feet high.

He remembers too, a dark beach and a moonlit sea at Bridlington. After an evening meeting for Christian boys, R. H. P. found a lad waiting outside the hall, struggling with his tears.

"What is the matter, Ted?" he asked.

"I'm not a Christian," answered the boy, "and I want to be one. I came hoping I should learn, but I felt so out of it. I haven't got any of the things you talked about."

"Let's go for a walk," said R. H. P.

So they went down to the shore and strolled along in the direction of Flamborough Head. All was dark ahead except for the gleam of the lighthouse, and behind them were the brilliant illuminations of Bridlington. R. H. P. preached Christ, and, standing beside the waves, Ted accepted Him.

As they turned back toward the town, Ted slipped his arm through that of his new friend and said, "Why, sir, that's just like me."

"Just like you? What do you mean, Ted?"

"Well, sir, you see, the darkness is all behind us now."

There was Billy, saved at a boys' meeting, and when saying goodbye he pressed a parcel into R. H. P.'s hand. "For you, sir," he mumbled.

"Oh, Billy," expostulated R. H. P., "you shouldn't waste your pocket-money on me!"

The answer was emphatic and spontaneous, "Sir, I can never repay."

Ballyholme, where a dear old lady trotted up after the beach service and asked, "Does your troupe perform all the summer, Mr. Pope?" Ballyholme, where a shining-eyed seven-year-old boy jumped over the pulpit right into R. H. P.'s arms and announced "Someone came to Jesus last night."

"Who was that?"

"Me!"

Ballyholme birthday, when he directed a musical evening with a children's choir trained by himself, with a talented young pianist whom he had led to the Lord accompanying. The children sang so beautifully that the audience parted almost in silence, and the evening has been remembered all down the years. R. H. P. sensed that the Spirit had been working, but with characteristic humility he went over to the pianist. "I think your fingers were consecrated tonight, Adrian," he said quietly.

Ballyholme in 1961, his last C.S.S.M. An old man, walking

slowly, but still the central, beloved figure. He had taken over the Ballyholme C.S.S.M. in 1932 from the Rev. Bryan Green, and the links of thirty years were strongly forged, and the influence of his work felt all over the district. He did not often speak, but when he did, his voice was as vibrant and strong as that of a young man. On the day of the birthday he was rowed across the bay in his proverbial white flannels and panama hat, to be dragged ashore by a crowd of excited children. But there was a great stilllness in the crowd, hundreds strong, as he mounted the pulpit and prayed, "We thank Thee, Lord, that the winds are quiet and they will not blow our words away. Thou didst command Peace, be still."

Sunday afternoon when he spoke on the text "Jesus Himself drew near" to the Emmaus disciples, to Joshua viewing Jericho, to the three men in the furnace, to Daniel in the lions' den. "The Lord was waiting for Daniel in that den," he said, half-musingly. " 'Daniel, I'm so glad you've come. You and I are going to spend such a happy night together.' Daniel spent a wonderful night with the Lord Jesus in that den." He finished with the oft-repeated story of the child who was asked the meaning of "I will never leave thee nor forsake thee," and who replied "It means that when there is one of us, there are always two of us."

After the service a shy little boy tugged at his coat and showed him a card. "You gave me that one year ago," he whispered, "do you remember why?" The incident pleased R. H. P. immensely, and his prayer that evening opened with an outburst of praise because a little boy had received Christ a year ago.

No account of his C.S.S.M. activities would be complete without mentioning the influence of his music. He wrote verse freely, and while most of it was doggerel, some is moving and beautiful, and his choruses are useful for their extreme simplicity and the way in which they say exactly what he wished them to say, no more and no less. As a musician he was extremely unorthodox, and the despair of those well-versed in theory and harmony. "You can't do that, Mr. Pope," they would say; to which he would reply triumphantly, "But I've done it!" and crash ahead. Occasionally his critics stood firm, and he was rather sorrowfully made to alter his productions. "I composed it," he explained later, "sitting at the piano, and Mrs. Archibald decomposed it!"

Nevertheless his tunes fitted his words, and perhaps few accompanists ever made children sing as he did, nor is there any doubt that his choruses caught on and remained in the minds of his little hearers all the way along.

"When I went to bed last night", wrote one, "I could not get to sleep. I kept saying to myself, 'Happy is the boy who believes in Him', over and over again, and, would you believe it, I woke in the middle of the night when it was pitch dark. Any other time I would have been afraid, but this time I knew I was with Jesus, and these words were on my lips, 'Happy is the boy . . .'"

"When I get home I sing 'shining all the time', and it seems to make mother and father and home delightful."

"When I'm in bed I sing all the choruses you learned me and mother says I don't half make a row."

He certainly had musical ability and a fair amount of confidence in his own powers. As a young man he was decidedly ambitious, and even started to compose an oratorio, while his operettas and comic songs were always an enormous success at boys' functions. But as life went on these exuberances lessened, and the choruses extant seemed to have been written very directly under God's guidance, often on the spur of the moment to fit a given subject.

"Into my heart" (No. 322 in Scripture Union *Chorus Book*) was written to be sung at the close of Canon King's address entitled 'House to Let', and who can say how many sang that prayer in deep sincerity that night?

At a boys' testimony meeting in Bristol in 1907 a shy lad rose to his feet and blurted out, "I accepted Jesus Christ this week, and . . . and . . ." His knees apparently gave way at this point and he sat down suddenly, but finished up valiantly from his seat, "it's simply grand!"

Other boys rose and spoke with greater fluency, but those words that had cost so much drummed in the leader's head, and at the close of the meeting he said he had a new chorus to teach them:

> Sin shall not have dominion over you!
> Oh, what a glorious message, and it's true.
> God has said it, it must stand;
> Pass it on, it's simply grand:
> Sin shall not have dominion over you.
>
> (No. 165 in Scripture Union *Chorus Book*)

After a meeting for very little boys at St. Andrews, Scotland, the audience crowded round the piano stool. "Make us a chorus just for us," they pleaded, and he complied immediately:

> I'm not too young to come to Jesus,
> For He loves a little child.

His 'Envelope talk' addressed to Many Mansions, Prepared Place, was well known and often repeated, but it gained considerably by the chorus he wrote to go with it, suggested by a remark of his wife's. The sun was setting one night, and she stood at the window gazing intently at a break in the clouds through which the very glory of God seemed to be shining.

"What are you thinking of, darling?" he asked.

"I was just thinking, how lovely to be there!" she replied.

They were going through a time of sore trial together, and he must have echoed the words. But not just yet! He must work a little longer, for he wanted more of the world's children to share that glory, and for them he wrote the chorus used at hundreds of subsequent meetings:

> Receive Him now, receive Him now,
> I will receive Him now.
> A place for me He will prepare,
> The joys of heaven with Him I'll share;
> And oh! how lovely to be there!
> I will receive Him now.

CHAPTER TEN

He Taught Others to Expect Conversions

R. H. P. thought much about the training of his workers and cared deeply about these young evangelists. His advice to them appeared in two books he wrote, entitled *To Teach Others Also,* and *Hints to Personal Workers.*

In 1953 he spoke at an Oxford breakfast held to recruit young men and women for the beach missions. The address, some of which is quoted below, shows how he stimulated the young to be up and doing. In his beach missions the men and women lived in separate house-parties. He was the last beach mission leader to adhere to this tradition, as he felt it made for greater concentration on the work in hand. Young and inexperienced they might be, but all must be truly converted, staunch believers in the divine inspiration of the Bible, and willing to work with all their might. As such, he saw no obstacle to any man becoming a soul-winner of children.

"All thinking people, whether holy or wicked, are agreed that the child is the most fertile soil in which to sow their seeds, whether of holiness or wickedness; and judging by the appearance of the harvest fields it would seem as though the wicked are working harder than the holy. I put it to you! How many of us have a sufficient sense of the importance of winning boys and girls for Christ to cause us to try to fit ourselves for this extremely important job? 'But,' says someone, 'I am no good with children.' Perhaps you have never tried; I believe that, given the spiritual drive and desire for their salvation the technique of controlling and speaking to boys and girls can be learned. The young medical student sees Sir Somebody, with half the alphabet after his name, perform a delicate operation. He says, 'I shouldn't be much good at that, but I intend to learn, and may be some day I shall outshine even Sir Somebody.'

"There are latent spiritual talents in many men which only need the touch of a child's hand to draw them forth. Has no child ever put his hand into yours and said, 'Lead me to Jesus?' Man, you have missed life's greatest thrill!

"No good with children! Do you not sometimes think into the future and humbly and reverently hope the day may come when some little folk may look up to you and call you Father? No good with children? Had you not better learn to be so, that if God in His wise love ever trusts any to your care you may not fail them, as so many parents do, at the most important point of all—their spiritual need? Some of you are going to be ordained. Must the teacher of your parish school say, as one said to me the other day, 'The vicar seldom comes to speak to us. He says he's no good with children, and I think he's right!'?"

The picture of him as a leader has to be built up from a number of thumb-nail sketches given by those who worked with him. Some of these are getting on in years now, and they look back with loving, grateful amusement, not unmixed with a sort of tired amazement as to how they ever kept up; for magnificent as he was in his organization of meetings, the organization of his programme was erratic in the extreme, and no one ever knew what he would be asked to do next. The schedule was as fluctuating as it was original. "Come on; let's have another boys' meeting!" he would remark exuberantly, when some were beginning to think about bed, and out would come the typewriter and all the paraphernalia for duplicating the invitations.

Yet they loved and revered him, and stuck to him year after year if they could, thanking God for the lessons learned from his dynamic, Spirit-filled leadership. They learned mostly from his life and example, for there was little time for much direct precept. His mind was mostly with the children, and his workers watched him, adopting his attitude, observing his methods, perhaps understanding something of his love for the Lord, and his secret burden for the souls of children, from which sprang his tremendous zeal and physical energy.

"How do you know what to do?" asked a nervous, prospective candidate.

"You don't," was the reply. "You just learn from Mr. Pope."

Many are the testimonies of his workers, and only a few can be selected, but they all tell much the same story.

"We learned to work," wrote one. "We worked every spare minute, and into the night to make a lighthouse for the birthday. Next afternoon R. H. P. called me and said, 'You know that lighthouse; could you turn it into a pagoda for missionary day?' We had only two days, but we did it, even if we did finish it off with cocoa when we ran out of brown paint just before midnight. On another occasion he wished to give a talk on Noah, and requested his workers to prepare a giant rainbow stretching a good twelve feet from side to side. But we knew that he worked harder than we did, and when at last we sank into bed after a day of work which had begun at 7 a.m. and lasted without pause or let up till night time, we would fall asleep to the sound of R. H. P.'s typewriter catching up on the correspondence. Often we woke to the same sound."

"We learned the value of prayer," wrote another, "and yet as one scans the programme one wonders at first where prayer came in. 'The mission itself is not the time for spending long hours in prayer,' he would reiterate. 'That should have been done before the mission.' Nevertheless his whole life was a close walk with God and one felt the presence of God as he gathered his whole party together morning and evening to pray."

"I remember him coming in one night completely worn out," wrote one worker; "nevertheless he took prayers, and his prayer consisted almost entirely of Scripture promises, as if, too tired to think, he threw himself back on God and His Word."

A stranger came in to one of these prayer meetings, and wrote to Mr. Pope afterwards:

"You and your happy band of workers made me realize how far I am from being a real Christian. I came to your prayer meeting last night. Can you tell me why I felt so desperately lonely at that meeting? I felt a tremendous barrier between myself and that earnest little group . . . there seemed to be a communion with a great, loving Friend in your midst, and as Jesus touched each one of you you poured forth your soul quietly and reverently."

"He understood us and stood by us," wrote another. "I remember a workers' prayer meeting at Criccieth. Mr. Pope spoke to us on the very practical side of Christianity, with the constant refrain, 'the devil's wedges have thin edges'. When he finished, we knelt to pray, but no prayer was spoken out loud. After a time of silence Mr. Pope closed in prayer. 'Lord,' he prayed, 'there are times when we cannot express the deepest desires of our hearts'."

He never asked his young workers to speak much. "Keep them back rather than push them forward," he once said. "The young must learn by example." But when they made their first efforts he trusted them, and very seldom criticized. "It would have to be something very serious for me to criticize," he once remarked. "How can I tell what the Holy Spirit told him to say?"

He helped them round their tight corners. The late Canon Guy King, as a young man, produced a huge model of an egg at a beach service. "Now, children, what is this?" he started brightly, but the model was so vast that the answers ranged from an airship to an asteroid. The situation was getting desperate, when a small voice piped up in front, "Please, sir, it's an egg." "Quite right, my boy," replied the speaker hastily in evident relief, not recognizing the voice as R. H. P.'s He was sitting, as usual, with the tinies, and hated to see one of his workers discomfited.

"He never asked anyone to do what he would not do himself," wrote another, and his capability must have sometimes made it hard for him to delegate. But, obvious and outstanding leader that he was, he would stoop to the humblest jobs. "There was poor old R. H. P. running all the errands," remarked a sympathetic visitor. "No one else he can really rely on yet!" And this difficulty was increased by the fact that, having trained his workers, he did not hold on to them for his own purposes. His policy was to send them on to other missions where their experience would count, while he himself started again. "I think you should go elsewhere next year," he said to a capable young man who had helped him three years running. He realized that the trainee was now ready for leadership.

One who worked with him, and who later wrote a Sunday school lesson book, prefaced it with these words:

"Dedication—to 'Dick' (R. Hudson Pope)

"I first learned from you how to preach the Gospel to young people. Since then you have taught me many lessons. What solemn times and what unrestrainedly jolly times we have spent together! But always I have left you with the sense that you brought me nearer to God. For the chief lesson you taught, and that in a hundred unsuspected ways, has been the lesson of Christlikeness. May I offer you this book as a token of my gratitude to God for your influence on my life and ministry."

The mood of the houseparty was swayed by his own. If the 'break' had not come, and children were not being saved, he was silent, withdrawn, like a man labouring under a heavy burden. But when the children began coming to Christ, his spirits soared to mercurial heights, carrying all before him. "I don't care if it snows blue puce!" he replied when the question of impossible weather was raised, and continued blithely with his project. At such times his humour was irrepressible. Mrs. Pope, who always accompanied him to the beach missions, would listen resignedly to these outbursts, but they had an agreement that if he told the same story too often at table she would balance her knife on her glass. At this signal he would subside and change the subject.

But on Saturdays a sort of week-end stillness would prevail, and he gathered his workers together for a quiet hour of teaching and exhortation. He dealt with such mundane, but, to him, immensely important, affairs as the discipline of the meeting-room—clean, attractive, well ventilated; the distance between the speaker and the children; the form of service. He reiterated his well-known rules of 'service technique'; the importance of the clear-cut, unmistakable command, distinct speech, punctuality and promptness of action. He taught them how to present the message of sin and salvation. "Get clear what you want to teach," he would say. "Consider who is in the audience. Let them know whether you are speaking to the saved or the unsaved. . . . What is your aim? What truths must we embody in every address? Will every address lead up to Christ?" He spoke with the utmost earnestness about the importance of a holy life, once defining it as follows:

Happy through the Word of God. Acts 28.39.
Obedient to the Will of God. Romans 7.5.
Lowly in the Way of God. Matthew 11.29.
Yielded to the Work of God. Romans 6.13.

These Saturday evening talks were a fitting preparation for a profitable Sunday, when workers walked to their own place of worship, and no vehicle was ever used, nor office work touched. Sometimes he read aloud to them and fed them with his own strong meat—Finney's *Revivals of Religion,* or *The Memoir and Remains of Robert Murray McCheyne.*

And, like himself, he taught them to expect conversions. "How many conversions are you expecting tonight?" he suddenly asked a young worker setting out to preach at a mission in the local church. The young man blushed. "Well, I don't know," he replied. Lovingly the older man turned to him and said with deep earnestness, "Go and expect some. If you don't expect, you'll never get!"

But supremely they learned his manner of dealing with children simply by watching him. "When I sit, as a parent, at the back of the service nowadays," wrote an old worker of his, "and see a young speaker leave the sand pulpit before the next has arrived, I seem to hear R. H. P.'s voice, clear above the crowd, 'By the time we have finished singing this chorus, Mr. Smith will be up here ready to talk to you'!" There, sitting on the sand among the children, they noted the perfect discipline, and saw how it was done. They heard those crystal-clear presentations of doctrine, they watched the rapt, lifted faces, arrested by his message. They sensed that quiet leading presence of the Holy Spirit leading on to a request for decisions, or holding back. They saw children convicted of sin and drawn to Christ by the love of the man in whom Christ dwelt. Those children flocked to him, and one never quite knew what he might do at the end of a meeting. He might be found surrounded by a crowd of little ones, nestling up to him in a quiet spot, or deep in conversation with some troubled boy. And once, when the readiness for personal work at the close of the service had been particularly stressed, an earnest young worker looked round to see just what R. H. P. was doing. He was standing on his head in the sand, accompanied by a couple of small, fair-haired twins.

CHAPTER ELEVEN

The Friend of Hundreds of Boys

R. H. P. was a lover of all children, but to him a boy was quite irresistible. He scented them out everywhere. "Come to the football match, and I'll find a boy to talk to," someone remembers him saying on Saturday afternoons, and we can be sure that he always did find a boy to talk to! He made friends with them on railway platforms, on trains, by the roadside, constantly asking God to guide him to them, as his own letters show.

He was always intensely interested in the Crusader Movement, in which his old friend Ted Olney had been one of the pioneers. He ran a mission for Crusader Classes in South London in 1913, and for many years he was leader of the Leeds Class. But owing to his frequent absences he resigned in favour of Mr. Alan Hepper, who had been converted through him as a boy, and was his beloved friend and co-worker all the way along.

"It is lovely being a fisher of boys", he wrote to Mr. Hepper, "and I'm sure the Lord honoured me very much in allowing me to catch a particularly big fish which has turned out to be a catcher also. I thank God on every remembrance of you, and may you keep on catching boys for Jesus."

In his frequent letters to this leader on the affairs of the class we get glimpses of R. H. P.'s great yearning that these boys should be their very best for God.

"I wrote a long letter to M. the other day. I covet him for the Lord's work, and put plainly about separation. He is a fine chap, and I long that he shall not become 'just an ordinary young man'. There are too many about of that type today."

"I *rejoice* at your news of the dear old Class, that the boys are hard at it with a boys' club. That is the thing to do. Get them saved, and then get them working . . . here is a suggestion for them in the summer holidays, that they should cycle out to the villages near at hand and have children's meetings . . . it could be a real work for them. Put it to them; where there is impression there must be expression, or else there will be compression, and something will have to go."

To their leader himself, he passed on all he could of his own experience and conclusions:

"You have had uphill work with the class, but it has been worthwhile work holding on. In a tug-of-war there is a time for heaving and pulling and a time for holding. The holding time is very trying sometimes and fairly pulls your muscles out, but sooner or later the enemy cannot bear the hold, and begins to show signs of yielding. Then comes the cry of 'heave', and heave we do, and away comes the handkerchief over the mark and the win is ours.

"I felt a new hope come into me as I looked again into the faces of those chaps at the last meeting. We must stick to them, we simply must, at all costs, and try to bring them through."

He resigned in 1929 from leadership of the Class with the greatest regret, but, as he wrote to Mr. Hepper,

"I do none of the work, come to few of the meetings, take none of the responsibility, and only make it more awkward for you having to consult me about things. . . . I know in the kindness of your heart you will say you want me to stay, and I appreciate your feelings to the full, but I do think that for the best interests of the class you should have it in your hands."

He was presented, on his resignation, with a beautiful leather address book, and a sincere, simply-worded testimonial of all that his leadership and teaching had meant. More precious still were some of the spontaneous replies sent in answer to his question, "What does Crusaders mean to you?"

"Being away from home," wrote one, "all sorts of temptations surround me. But I have only to look down at my badge and think of the time I found God."

"I don't think I have ever come away from a meeting without feeling keener, or realizing the joy of my salvation," wrote another.

Later on, he became deeply interested in the Stockton-on-Tees Crusaders, and wrote frequently to their leader Alwyn Harland. In the midst of all the pressure and claims of his own missions he wrote in loving detail about all that went on in that class, although he was probably seldom there in person.

"How lovely about J. E. and all those others. You will certainly have your hands full looking after all these young plants. I often feel glad in this connection that our Lord said 'My Father is the husbandman' . . . Thanks for the list of boys. I do hope and pray they are all following on to know the Lord. . . . I am anxious to know what further answer to prayer there was re A. M."

In later years still, he worked unsparingly for the Harrogate Crusaders, and he was deeply burdened for them and offered up his failing strength in love and prayer for them to the end. But while this deep travail of soul for their spiritual welfare was probably beyond their comprehension, there was, over and above it all, a fatherly concern and understanding to which they almost invariably responded. The burdened in spirit are not always the easiest to talk to, but outwardly he lived at their level, and they all knew that he loved them. He enjoyed their company, he laughed at their jokes, he shared their interests, and sympathized with their difficulties. And the proverbially reserved teenagers opened up to him with amazing frankness, recognizing in him one who was not only longing to lead them to Christ, but to be their friend and counsellor all through their adolescence.

Not that his straight, hard-hitting messages were always acceptable or popular. They were too uncompromising for the half-hearted.

"I gather from what you say", he wrote to one leader, "that after my last visit class attendance went down. If this is because the Lord is dealing with people, then I am not grieved. But if, as is most likely, it was because I gave the message in a clumsy way, then I am indeed sorry."

Critical letters, even rude letters, reached him in plenty, but each was answered courteously and painstakingly, although he could speak very sternly if God's Word was attacked. At a testimony meeting one night, an older boy rose, and in a clever ten-minute speech he scoffed at the whole idea of salvation. R. H. P. listened quietly, and then rose, undisturbed, to his feet. "We've just had a testimony for the devil," he said, "now let's have one for the Lord." And it was because of the sorry contrast of that adverse testimony that one thoughtful schoolgirl decided for Christ that night.

But letters of another kind reached him by the hundreds—letters from schoolboys, mostly too private for publication, pouring out their hearts to this wise, understanding friend. Their temptations, failures, spiritual longings and achievements mingle, rather surprisingly sometimes, with the cricket score, the tuck-shop, and the doings of white rabbits. Sad to say, the replies to these screeds have not usually been preserved, but how they fortified their readers in the good fight against cheating, impurity, irreverence, slackness, profanity, doubt, and wrong friendships, as some of the acknowledgments show.

"Your message to us at camp, 'Have you got a bad conscience, a bad habit, a bad friend?', so moved me that after the meeting I went and apologized to a boy for the way I had treated him. He did the same to me, and since that day we've been inseparable."

"You have no idea how pleased I was to get your letter. Satan has got his sixteen-inch guns and bombing planes trained on me just now, and I need all the reinforcements I can get. I've suffered many defeats in my Christian life, and to get a letter from you was like a ray of sunshine."

The ensuing list of problems in this last letter would have required a very long reply to deal with them, but no doubt that reply was written. It is probably true to say that no letter was ever left unanswered, although just how, we wonder, did he deal with the following?

"Do you think it would be a good idea to make a list of as many bad things as I could, and take, say, one every week or until I thought I'd conquered it, and then cross it off the list, but still keep my eye on it? Say I conquered meanness, the list would be like this:

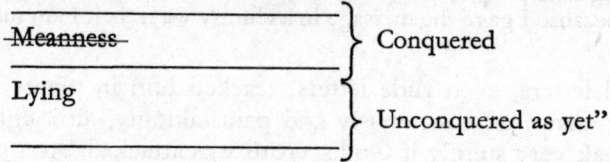

He had hundreds of talks with boys, collectively and individually, and wrote a number of booklets on the subject of clean, straight living. He knew how to touch a conscience and reach down to the dregs of a life, and yet no one ever felt that he despised him or was shocked by his confession; only gladdened by the repentance and eager for victory.

"You know the chorus we sang about a good friend knows the worst about you and loves you just the same," ran one letter, particularly innocent of punctuation, "there is only one Jesus is His name well there is two because you know the worst about me and still like me at least I hope you do."

"I suppose if I were to say that before you came I was deep down in shameland, fighting in my own strength but falling deeper into sin, it would be true, and I the secretary . . . the one supposed to teach others; could anything be more appalling? I went home and knelt in prayer long after everyone was in bed and then I distinctly heard Him say, 'Son, be of good cheer, thy sins be forgiven thee . . .' I have been gloriously triumphant ever since, and I cannot be grateful enough to you for speaking so plainly and leading me home."

In one of the last meetings he ever held for boys, when he was well over eighty, he took the subject of the Good Samaritan, and gave a clarion warning of the danger of sin in a young life. The talk is reproduced in note form only, and the writer was allowed to sit at the back and listen. As a rule, when R. H. P. spoke to boys there were no spectators present.

"He tried to travel from Jerusalem to Jericho alone and unarmed —no sword or stick, and he was carrying valuables. Had no one warned the foolish man? Perhaps he was too proud. Perhaps he just didn't know it was dangerous.

"The early teens are a time of great danger—I have spoken to two boys recently. One was fourteen, and his eyes filled with tears at the end of a talk. 'Sir,' he said, 'why didn't someone tell me all this two years ago?' The second was fifteen, and I said to him, 'Jim, the seas will soon get rough.' 'I know,' he replied, 'but I'm not steering the boat.'

"There are robbers lying in wait on a seemingly attractive path. Sin is very subtle and has many disguises. The cut-worm gnaws through a strong growing stalk half an inch underground. No one knows what is happening until the stalk suddenly falls. And these robbers are lurking all round us, unseen, unrecognized.

"There is one who robs reverence. 'Could I be saved?' asked a boy of eleven on the last night of a mission. 'I've been out every night and made fun of the service.'

"There is one who cuts away uprightness by lying and cheating; there is another who cuts away self-control by smoking, swearing, drinking and self-indulgence. 'I've tried to give it up,' cried a boy in despair, 'but now it won't give me up.' A young factory worker thought he would try a larger machine than his own. His coat was caught in the wheel and he was dragged to his death. It was easy to set the machine in motion, but too late did he realize that he didn't know how to stop it.

"There is the robber of purity. A boy heard a solemn warning at fourteen, and refused it. At the age of twenty-one he sent a telegram to the one who had pleaded with him, asking for an interview. Few would have recognized in the bitter face the bright schoolboy of seven years previously. In his hand was a letter from the man who had led him astray and whose advice he had also asked in that hour of crisis. It said, 'Don't worry; it will probably come out right, and if it doesn't you can always shoot yourself.'

"The robbers will come. Perhaps you are already robbed and wounded; but you need not perish. The Good Samaritan is here tonight to pardon confessed sin. You can be cured ... carried ... cared for ... called for.

"Some boy may say, 'These robbers have never attacked me', but *they will come,* so don't start on the journey alone. Had that man had a friend it would never have happened, but he started alone. You are carrying very valuable things—a clean mind, a clean conscience, a good influence, and if you start with Christ you need never lose them.

"Sixty-nine years ago I took Him as my Guide, and He's never left my side. I've failed, but He's picked me up. We need a Saviour to pull us out of the ditch. We need a Saviour to hold our hand, so that we shall not fall into the ditch. You can put your hand in His and go away tonight.

"A Swiss guide was once leading a party across a glacier. He jumped across a crevasse and helped them over one by one. The last was left, and she looked down into the blue depths and shuddered. 'It's no good,' she said, 'I can't jump it!' 'Madam,' replied the guide, 'this hand has been helping people over crevasses for twenty-five years, and it's never let anyone fall yet. Won't you trust me?'

"The hand of the Lord Jesus has been helping boys for two thousand years, and it's never let go of one yet. ... I can't take you any further. The rest must be between you and God."

The meeting closed with the singing of a hymn. Most of the boys in the room were Christians, but at least one unconverted lad came to Christ that night.

His boys wrote to him, not only about their sins and temptations, but about their hopes and joys as well.

"God seems to be helping me at school this term because I am getting much better marks. He also seems to be helping me in games, because I am getting a lot more wickets with my bowling."

"I am feeling very much better after that talk and am feeling happy; there is going to be a paper chase, it will be so jolly, I'm going to be a hare."

Reginald Wallis, converted through him at the age of fourteen, wrote pages and pages of boyish scrawl:

"I keep on telling them at home, not one of my uncles beats dear old Uncle Dick. Write when you get a spare five minutes. You know how encouraging it is for me to receive a letter from my dear old uncle who gave me that ever memorable day. We are two brothers both converted by the same text at the same age."

"I asked you to pray that I might surrender all," wrote a senior boy. "Praise God, your prayer has been answered. Now pray I may get my body really fit. I'm going in for the mile, and I'm going in for that to the full. I can't do this without Christ's help."

The series of letters from this boy, who died as a young man, reveal a remarkably swift growth in spiritual maturity, and no doubt this was partly due to the faithful replies and prayers of the friend to whom he wrote them. All was joyfully shared:

"We have had some grand p.m.s. this term. Many boys pray regularly now, and their prayers are earnest and practical. Every side of our lives is brought before God at these meetings. Sometimes I make a point of praying for purity and honesty, and another boy will praise God for a fresh realization of the Cross, another will ask for the gift of the Holy Spirit, another for the meetings we hold, another for help in lessons, and another for a more peaceful disposition . . . you would like it! . . . do pray for me, I nearly get desperate sometimes . . . you *are* good to me, Mr. Pope, I can never repay what you've done for me."

Just a few of the letters which so cheered these young warriors have been treasured over the years, as he treasured theirs.

"You want to help boys to know Jesus, you want to be used of God, you want to lead the finest life you can; then cut clear of the old sinking ship entirely, and of anything that you might love better than you love your Lord. As you grow older you will be a thousand times glad that you made a clean sweep of the whole lot and did not trifle away any of the precious hours that you might have been using in His service."

"You cannot slide into high spiritual experience," he wrote to a young man about to start in business. "You must climb to it. You cannot drift into a working knowledge of your Bible. It must be slogged at, and nothing must be allowed to stand in the way if you are to be a godly man. Business is important, but to give God and His Word their place will not interfere with proper business, but will rather fit you for it and make it easier. William Carey used to say, 'My business in life is to win souls for Christ. I cobble soles to pay expenses.' Your business in life is to save souls, and you will survey to pay expenses. The first purpose for which God put you into this world is to be a soul-winner, and the second is to be a soul-winner, and the ultimate end of your existence is to be a soul-winner. Incidentally, you will have to work hard and well to pay expenses, but remember what you are here for. The world says, 'He that winneth money is wise'. God says, 'He that winneth souls is wise'."

And not only boys, but parents and schoolmasters, praised God for R. H. P.'s influence.

"Thank you deep down for your offensive, 'Thou shouldest not have looked on', wrote the headmaster of a famous grammar school. "It is a great text and just what we need. If we can turn these spectators into the ring and get them to take their coats off and do a bit of brave sparring, we shan't be wrong. It is due to 'looking on' that gambling, dirt, drink and profanity flourish in our midst.... I want to say thank you, and God will reward you. Many of our lads have found what is of more value than all the learning in the world."

"Into the ring"—"coats off"—"brave sparring"! He would have liked that, for he taught them to be fighters. And sometimes, like one who signs himself Tame Beaver, they took him literally: "It is not at all hard for me to be a Christian, for if anyone dares say anything wrong about religion, I knock him down!"

CHAPTER TWELVE

"Another Member Sends 4d."

THE Scripture Union, started in 1867, has now become an international Bible reading movement with a membership of more than a million and a quarter members from all over the world. Mr. Pope had his own personal Scripture Union branch known as 'the Dead Keen Branch', and at his retirement this numbered about 900 members, to whom he personally sent out annual mottoes and cards. As the years went by, some dropped off, but he never dropped them; unacknowledged and unpaid he continued to send, and often his very persistence overcame them, and they would write an apologetic letter of thanks with a postal order enclosed. The office work and correspondence involved was very heavy, and it seems incredible how he managed to fit it into a life already so crowded with missions and commitments.

Most of the members of his personal branch were drawn from public and preparatory schools, in about eighteen of which he had conducted regular meetings out of school hours. They were not quite the same style of meeting as his evangelistic missions, his subject being the Word of God and the Scripture Union. "Talk about the Scripture Union and stick to it," was his advice. "Don't make it a springboard for other subjects," and certainly some of his finest talks were based on the subject of the Bible. After the meeting, he would take the names, ages and addresses of those interested, and send them their cards, filled up in his own handwriting, their notes and their badges. If the boy or girl had no Bible and found it difficult to obtain one, he would provide one, as he did in answer to the following surprising appeal, written in very young handwriting, after a talk on Jesus blessing the children:

> 'I am now a Christian who sat on God's knee. I have no Bible Mother has serched the house with a toothcoome but she cannot find a bible."

It is interesting to follow up those Scripture Union meetings in schools and to trace the growth of some of the branches left to the inexperienced leadership of boys. One is often amazed at the strength and persistence of their first love for the Lord, and, of course, letters poured in, and all were answered at length. 'Mike' seems to have been a formidable character:

> "Just a line to let you know I have enlisted another member who sends 4d. I doubt if we shall find many more members now, for we have about cleared off the school except for a few boys who rather correspond to non-conformists."

And from the same school address comes another testimony to this remarkable effort:

> "C. has just joined, he seems to be a realy nice sort of boy, generous and kind and I am shure he will take Jesus into his house or temple or body. The S.U. is realy making a difference in the school and chapps who used the popuorlarity in a bad way now use it to help those who need it and it has really been the making of R-2."

And of course they met with bitter disappointments, and these too had to be shared in letters:

> "It's an absolute failure about the S.U. cards. Everyone wants them till you say how much they are and then they say 'no thanks'. It is awfully difficult to make any one buy them, and you get jeered at, and it does make one feel rotten, but I'll stick to it and go on trying."

But whether they started groups or not, what the habit of daily Bible reading means in the life of a child cannot be overestimated. How much it must have meant to the lonely child who wrote:

> "I am glad to see another S.U. card, it is a sign that we are a year nearer to God. I will try my hardest to get some new members. I am alone with God at school because Stephen has left.
>
> "Every morning I read my Bible," wrote a young garage apprentice, "and that short period seems to freshen me up to fight the good fight.
>
> "I have wonderful news for you," wrote a grammar school boy. "For the first time in my life I have brought a sinner to God. He was crying because his friend had died, and I showed him the text Matthew 5.4, 'They that mourn shall be comforted'. He straightway felt better, so I read him the Scripture Union portion which cheered him up. Later he said, 'My life has been changed' and he prayed with me. I do thank you for bringing me to Jesus. He and I thank you very much."

So the letters continued to pour in. Was he ever baffled by the enormous diversity of problems he was expected to solve? Apparently not, for every one is marked 'Rep', although sometimes people did expect a lot of him!

"Please pray for my grandfather. He is dead and I want him to come back to me."

"Please explain to me the book of Ezekiel."

A friend recalls him sometimes sitting silent at his typewriter for an hour or more, head bowed, just praying or pondering over some problem—the cry for help of a young man wrestling with doubt and agnosticism, or the appeal of some lonely little Christian child needing help. To each he gave his whole heart and mind. The following, taken at random, are specimens of what he would sit down to deal with at the end of a hard day's work.

"Our prayer meeting is going splendidly the attendance averages 45. But one or two boys pray for too long and repeat. What can I do? It would be awful to ask them to be shorter, wouldn't it? Can you let me know on a postcard?"

A long letter from an undergraduate:

"If God is omnipotent why does He allow so much needless suffering to go on? His love is very hard to find. What reward do the faithful get, if any? Or do they have to die first, and anyway what is death? It doesn't seem fair that God should make human beings, who never asked to be born, go through such misery and then chuck them into hell at the end. . . . Either He can't put evil away, or He wants to give us a hard time. In either case He doesn't seem worth trusting. If you can give me some ground for faith and save me from agnosticism I'd be glad if you'd try. Please help me . . . I'm beginning to think God has gone away and left me, and unless someone conclusively proves He has not I shall go on in that belief."

"I hope I have Jesus as my Saviour," wrote a younger boy. "I don't go round thinking of Him all day long, but I'm a jolly sight better than I used to be. Please write and tell me how I stand toward my Saviour. This is a funny letter, but it is a turning point in my life. Reading the booklet was the first stage. Reading your letter and thinking about myself was the second stage. The third will be when I get your next letter." I've just been kicked for telling a chap he's desecrating the sabbath, so I'm just going to tell him again. Please write and say if this is the right way. I don't quite know."

"I'm feeling down in the dumps. My faith in God is wobbly, and I've told some dirty jokes. Please write and set my feet on the Rock."

Or this, on a postcard:

"I am writing to ask advice because things aren't going well. A cocky and conceited spirit has siezed me and I am resolved to fight it."

His replies to such letters sometimes covered pages. Eight typed pages were sent to a boy who wanted assurance of salvation, and the following treasured reply was sent to a boy whose friend had asked him to prove the existence of God:

"I do not think you can prove the existence of God except by consistent behaviour. Much depends on why he asked the question. If he is in earnest to know, because he wants to serve God and obey Him, then God will certainly reveal Himself. But, alas, most who ask this question are doing so out of idle curiosity. The fact is God is a very inconvenient person to have about if one wants to go on one's own way and continue in sin. I have found that very often people who say there is no God do so because there is some particular sin they do not wish to part with, and the only way to have peace of mind about it is to force themselves into believing that God does not exist.

"The Bible claims to reveal God. Let your friend take his Bible and prayerfully study it, and with set purpose go on studying it, until he does find God. If he won't do this, then no amount of argument will convince him. Further, to find God your friend must closely study the life and words of the Lord Jesus, for He said in Matthew 11.27, "Neither knoweth any man the Father save the Son, and he to whomsoever the Son will reveal Him." Jesus is the only way to God, so your friend will have to come face to face with Jesus. No man can ignore Christ and find God. 'Nothing is easier than for someone to say, 'Prove to me that there is a God', and to expect an answer in some trite little sentence. It isn't done that way. Christ reveals God and the Bible reveals Christ, so the way is open to your friend. But if he will not seek God in God's appointed way, he will never find Him until he meets Him at the judgment seat. Then how foolish will sound his excuse, 'No one proved to me that there was a God'."

Perhaps after a pile of correspondence of this type he would turn with weary relief to the little blotted, mis-spelt ones:

"I am earnestly seeking Jesus, and I should like a letter telling me how to become a little servant of Jesus."

"We are going to make a wigwam of dead sticks. Our cat loves a teddy bear to play with. I wish you were here. Do you think a book called *The Pirates of Eldorado*, price 3d., will hurt me? I'm not quite sure."

"Mr. Pope, when Jesus opens my eyes, can they shut again? Please answer this in a little letter."

"Mr. Pope, I have now got to work for Jesus, but I don't know what to do. Please write and tell me."

"Another Member Sends 4d."

"While you have been in this district you have converted at least one sinner to Jesus. Mr. Pope, I want to hear thing after thing about God."

CHAPTER THIRTEEN

Never Under-rate the Under-eights

"NEVER under-rate the under-eights," was one of R. H. P.'s favourite working principles. He believed that real, lasting conversion to God was possible at an exceedingly early age.

"You have made me an honest Christian," wrote one child. "Is my brother too young? He is two."

R. H. P.'s reply is not recorded, but he was probably not too damping! He insisted that he had personally known children of three accept Christ, and that the subsequent years had proved that their faith and understanding had been real. He often recalled sitting under a table in an air raid with a child of four whose father had gone out on warden work. The little thing seemed frightened until it remembered some talk it had had with Mr. Pope. Then it sang 'I'm H-A-P-P-Y' with great content, until it fell asleep.

Others may doubt the reality of this, and some strongly disagreed with him. A father once came to him on the sands and remonstrated with him:

"My son is very young for what you speak of—conversion," he complained.

"Is he too young to sin?"

"No."

"Then I don't think he's too young to need a Saviour."

The fact remained that lasting results were frequently seen in little children. Ben, aged eight, came to a meeting and behaved very badly. He was turned out, so the next night he amused himself by throwing stones on the corrugated roof of the building. A window was broken, frightening the children, and the meeting ended in confusion. The organizer suggested sending for the Police, for Ben was a very difficult child, and even the Salvation Army had given him up as hopeless.

"Wait one more day," said R. H. P., and he re-arranged the hall, turning the chairs in another direction. Then he bought a boys' paper called *The Captain,* labelled it "Ben, with love from Mr. Pope", and dropped it in at Ben's front door.

That evening Ben was at the meeting in his Sunday suit, quiet and serious. At the close he asked if he might stay on for the next meeting, which was for boys of over fourteen.

"Has God been speaking to you, Ben?" asked Mr. Pope.

"Yes, sir, He has," answered the child, and with what R. H. P. termed "a special dispensation from the Pope" Ben sat through the next gathering and came to the Saviour at the end of it. R. H. P. kept up with him for years, and he grew into a steady Christian boy.

Jim accepted Christ at the age of six, at the close of a beach service. A year later he sought out Mr. Pope. He had no doubts as to his salvation, but he had a problem. "How can I stop telling lies to Daddy?"

"Be filled with the Spirit," said R. H. P. seriously to the troubled seven-year-old. "Then when Mr. Liar comes to the door you will simply look out of the top window and say 'House full'. "

Some years later Jim was there again. "I'm getting too cocksure of myself," he complained. "What can I do about it?"

"Exactly the same as you did about the lies," answered R. H. P. "Be filled with the Spirit."

"A little child needs a little child's Saviour" was another of his favourite slogans, and he firmly believed that the Lord would meet them at the level of their need, however small that need might appear from grown-up heights.

And just how much had five-year-old John grasped when he attended his first beach service in August and learned the chorus "Into my heart"? He said nothing at the time, but at Christmas he was given a gaily-painted set of the Big Bad Wolf and the three little pigs. Great was his delight, and he loved to inform the pigs that even the thought of them made the wolf's mouth water. Every precaution was taken to keep them apart, and at night they were carefully stored in separate boxes.

But one night the small face was thoughtful and he informed his mother that wolf and pigs could all sleep in the same box. "He's not a big bad wolf any longer, Mummy," he explained. "He's a big good wolf. He's been singing what we sang on the beach,

'Into my heart', and he's changed, Mummy. He doesn't want to eat them any longer. He loves them."

"The Scripture fixes no age for conversion", wrote R. H. P., "and neither must we, seeing it is a matter of revelation, 'when it pleased God to reveal His Son in me'. He can do this at any age, and this is why it is so important to teach the child the great doctrines of the Bible from the very cradle. It will give the Holy Spirit something on which to work.

"Polycarp, Isaac Watts, Lord Shaftesbury, were all converted between the ages of seven and ten. We must not limit the power of God in this matter. If a child is old enough to sin, and old enough to die, it would be a strange thing if he were not old enough to be saved."

They recognized his love and loved him in return, and as little children usually recognize the divine through the human, that love drew them to Jesus as they flocked round him on the sands or sat on his knee. A seven-year-old climbed into his lap and remarked later to his mother, "I love everything about him except his moustache prickles".

The little tokens of their love were treasured by him, and he often told of a very small boy who handed him a penny just as his train was leaving. "For the mission," he said. And in his old age he carried about with him a white silk book-marker with 'God' embroidered on it in straggling, irregular letters. The story was as follows:

A tiny child wanted to make him a present.

"I want to send him a message on this book-marker," he said.

"What do you want to write?"

"God is love."

"But there isn't room."

"Well, Mummy, wouldn't there just be room for God?"

There was!

His gift of explaining deep truth to the very young is well known, and he insisted they must have it, and gave it them by the hour. The length of his addresses was proverbial, but it was the parents who objected, not the children, and he took very little heed of adult objections. Once, when publicly presented by a member of his house party with a pair of scissors "with which to cut the length of your addresses", he replied calmly that, on the contrary, they had given him two extra points! In fact, it was a habit he never attempted to correct, and he would say to the children, "Now, I still want to tell you one more thing. And if Mother says you're late, say, 'It's not my fault. It's that funny old man's fault, he went on talking and talking!'"

A matter of life and death, he would say, must not be cramped for time, and the children were with him all along. They would sit absorbed, following him up paths of truth where they had probably never walked before, understanding clearly probably for the first time in their lives the doctrines that few people ever attempt to explain to small children; and hearing them vitally connected to their small problems and fears.

"State the truth in Scripture language," he would say; "explain to the best of your ability, and leave the Holy Spirit to do the rest."

> "I sometimes wonder", he commented, "whether those who object to telling the story of the Crucifixion to little children have ever had any deep experience of its meaning in their lives. I cannot help feeling that if they had, they could not leave it out of their teaching. There is nothing gruesome in the way the narrative is told in the Bible, so why not tell little children just what the Bible says? I never remember a little child being shocked or upset by the story of the Cross. I have seen many weep because they have not loved the Saviour Who did all that for them. But these are precious tears, and God wipes them away with His heavenly handkerchief of love and forgiveness. We have a solemn responsibility, for we are laying foundations for all future teaching. Let us give our little ones the truth, the whole truth, and nothing but the truth, but do it with the tender love and happy winsomeness with which the Lord Jesus won your own heart to Himself."

Sin and *conviction* he loved to illustrate by three books: "My book—others' book—God's book", and would speak on what sin does to me, what it does to others, what it did to Christ. There were three kinds of sin—secret sin, open sin, and the great sin, that of refusing Jesus as the Sin-Bearer.

For *Faith* he used his old acrostic "Forsaking All I Take Him", and linked it with a second acrostic "Jesus Exactly Suits Us Sinners". He would then pass on to *Regeneration*, children who are born again, and children who are not born again. *Salvation* included justification, sanctification and glorification, and is 'God's birthday present' to the believer and receiver. "By justification I was saved. By sanctification I am being saved. By glorification I shall be saved." R. H. P. called them more simply His pardon, His power, His presence, and he once based a talk for boys on the following theme:

His pardon saves from a bad conscience.
His power saves from bad habits.
His presence saves from bad companions.

Substitution, he insisted, needed great care, lest an unsaved person should think that if Jesus died as a substitute for all, were not all saved? He often illustrated this with the Passover story. "The son looks at the sprinkled blood and says, 'The lamb has died to make it possible for me to be saved.' If, however, he remains outside the door he will perish, in spite of the lamb having died. But if in faith he steps inside the house, then, as he marches off with the others in the morning, he can say, 'The lamb died instead of me'."

He seldom overlooked *predestination,* a subject most children's evangelists would probably avoid like the plague!

"When I talk to a child," he said, "I often say, 'Do you know why you have come to Christ?'

" 'No, sir', the child answers.

" 'Well, I will tell you', I say. 'You have come because you are one of those whom God gave to Christ. Long ago, before you were born, God said, "I am going to give that child to Christ, and one day that child will come to Him." By coming you have proved this. You are God's present to the Lord Jesus.' "

Heaven and Hell he explained simply as the presence or absence of Jesus. To be with Jesus in heaven, for He said to His friends "Where I am there ye shall be also". To be without Jesus is hell, for He said to His enemies "Whither I go ye cannot come".

To worried children who wondered whether they could 'keep it up' he would reply, "You haven't got to keep Him, He is keeping you", and would imitate with delightful effect a conversation between two sheep. "Ba-a-a," said the lamb, "I'm so afraid I shan't be able to keep my shepherd." "Ba-ba," replied the sheep, "don't be silly. You aren't keeping the shepherd. The shepherd is keeping you."

Yet in spite of all his simplicity they did occasionally misunderstand.

"Do I have to cut myself open here to let Jesus into my heart?" asked six-year-old Robin anxiously, laying a small hand on his chest.

"Robin," asked R. H. P., "have I got a place in your heart?"

There was no doubt about the answer to that. Robin's troubled face brightened and he nodded vigorously.

"Well, how did I get in?"

"When I began to love you."

"That is how Jesus comes in. If any man love Me . . . We will come to him."

"To teach simply," he would often reiterate, "you must know deeply."

CHAPTER FOURTEEN

God's Gentleness Made Him Great

MR. POPE had always been unconcerned as to the size of a meeting. There was a day when his lantern talk on the Life of Christ clashed with some school event, and one rather embarrassed lad turned up, and sat with four or five disappointed workers, in the otherwise empty hall. R. H. P. quietly carried on, and preached as usual with all his heart and soul, and the boy was converted.

Nor would he ever, if humanly possible, cancel a meeting. One wild winter's night the snow was falling so thickly in Lancashire that those responsible for the meeting presumed that no one would turn up. Not so R. H. P. He packed a dozen boys into the car and drove to the hall bringing his audience with him. At the end of the meeting one boy, called Baker, stayed on, sobbing bitterly, under deep conviction of sin. He accepted Christ and became a fine Christian. Years later, when the battleship Graf Spee attacked a small cargo boat, the Chinese crew panicked, but Baker took over the wheel until a shell blew the bridge to pieces. Sudden death meant sudden glory, because of a meeting which most missioners would have given up.

The little meeting was to him just as important as the big one, because he never saw people *en masse*—at least, certainly not children. "You may speak to half a dozen children in an evening," he said, "but will you remember this? While the fifth one is number five to you, he himself is not one of a number. To him it is *the* crisis of his life. You are not getting rid of them in batches. To each one of the six it may be their supreme moment, so never get used to doing it."

So to him, faithful in that which was least, was entrusted a wider ministry, and in 1960, at the age of eighty-one, Mr. Pope was asked to speak at Keswick. Frail, but still immensely virile on the platform, he took a number of smaller meetings during his stay and gave one address in the big tent to the assembled Convention. Perhaps they expected him to speak on his usual theme, his work among children, and to pass on the experience of his long and fruitful life, but the subject he did choose must have been a surprise to some. He spoke on "The Most Expensive Thing in the World"—the infinite costliness of sin in a believer. It was a last great solemn warning and entreaty, "that ye sin not".

And this again explains the secret of his power and strength with God and man—his fear and hatred of sin. "Light, obedience. More light, more obedience. Further light and further obedience." That was the rule of his life. Sin to him was not just failure or weakness or carelessness; it was disobedience, and he carried his obedience into every detail of his daily life.

"Remember the Sabbath day to keep it holy", says the Word, and all his life he kept Sunday strictly however much inconvenience it might involve. The truth of "them that honour Me I will honour", was shown in the following incident, as related by one who was present.

"Open air meetings had been held during the summer in the market-place at Harrogate. Toward the end of the season, R. H. P. suggested we should have a lantern lecture instead, and take advantage of the darker evenings.

"The suggestion was received somewhat cautiously. All sorts of problems loomed in our minds. R. H. P. was known as a strict sabbatarian; how were we going to get all the equipment on the spot on a Sunday evening? True, it would be dark by 8 p.m., but what about the glare from the shop windows with their fluorescent lighting? Again, ten-minute testimonies would hold a passing audience, but would an hour long lecture hold the people?

"It was decided to go on with the idea. I broached the subject of equipment with Mr. Pope and suggested that I would get someone to call with a car for lantern, table, screen and frame, etc. R. H. P. said, 'I've my own car if we wanted to do it that way. We must pray that God will show us His way.' Then I spilled all my difficulties about shop lights, etc. 'Go home,' said R. H. P., 'and pray about these things and meet me at the market place on Friday at 3 p.m.'

"Friday came and I kept the appointment. First we tackled the shop lighting problem. R. H. P. disclosed his plan of action. 'You will go along all the shops on that side and ask them courteously to arrange to darken their windows on Sunday evening. I will do the same along this side.' My first shop was an immediate success. 'Of course we will drop our blind on Sunday evening.' The next shop, a herbalist's, had no blinds, and his lighting was on a time switch which was sealed. After some conversation the owner said, 'The only

H

way I could help would be if I came myself and opened the shop to put the power off at the mains.' There was a moment's hesitation, and then he came down in our favour. He not only came to put off his lights, he stayed for much of the meeting. Enough to say that every shop on both sides of the street had lights out.

"Now there was the question of electricity supply. R. H. P., always the Christian gentleman, went into a shoe repair shop, and very soon the cobbler had steps out opening a little fanlight window above his shop. He would fit an adaptor to his light, lead the wire out through the fanlight, and all we would have to do would be to plug in.

"Then there was the transport problem. Mr. Pope took me round a back lane. 'There's a potato warehouse somewhere here,' he said, 'I think we shall get help,' We did, and it was delightful to hear R. H. P. explain that we would like our stuff on the spot rather than desecrate God's day. Yes, of course, it would be all right! We could leave our goods there on Saturday and collect them again on Monday. 'How do we get them out on Sunday?' I asked. To which the manager replied, 'That's simple. I'll give Mr. Pope the key.'

"Sunday night came. Everything worked according to plan, and a good audience heard the Life of Christ in the words of Scripture."

"Swear not at all," says the Book, and how tremendously seriously he urged Christians to keep the door of their lips.

"All those who are to be faithful workers for the Lord must learn to govern their tongues," he said. "A Christian does not curse, but would it not be a good thing if we could avoid getting near it? Darn, drat, blow, hang!... every idle word that men shall speak, they shall give account thereof in the day of judgment."

A naturally gifted, self-opinionated young man, with a certain amount of self-confidence and a rapidly growing reputation as an extremely successful evangelist, he learned, as the years passed, to fear pride as he feared the devil himself.

"Oh the temptations that come pouring into the life of a man or a woman who means to have a faithful ministry for the Lord!" he cried. "There is pride over and over again. 'How beautifully I did that address!' 'How wonderfully the children listened!' Pride will spoil everything if we let it come in."

Right to the end he fought it. "If others do better than we, don't let us get jealous," he prayed brokenly at his last C.S.S.M. "Keep us from pride. We are so weak... so weak." But that constant sense of weakness kept him ever leaning, and that extreme sensitiveness to sin wrought in him a growing wonder at the love and forgiveness of his Saviour. "To whom much is given the same loveth much", and often in his old age he would break out into the following lines:

> He didn't wait till I came to Him,
> But He loved me at my worst.
> He needn't ever have died for me
> If I could have loved Him first.
> For it wasn't that I might spend my days
> Just in work or sin or strife
> That Jesus, the Son of God, has given
> His love, and laid down His life.
> It wasn't that I might spend my life
> Just as my life's been spent
> That He brought me so near to His mighty cross,
> And has told me what it meant.
> He doesn't need me to die for Him,
> He only asks me to live,
> There's nothing of mine He wants but my heart,
> And it's all that I've got to give.

Stern and uncompromising to the slightest deviation from obedience, yet life taught him to be wonderfully gentle to the seeker, and, as years passed, very humble toward those who disagreed with him.

On his desk at Harrogate there stood a text. "I could have been burdensome . . . I was gentle"—so gentle that little children could whisper, or spell out, their secrets without fear or shyness, and sinners could show him all their shame. Truly God's gentleness had made him great!

CHAPTER FIFTEEN

The Joy of Arrival

In Harrogate there was a house much frequented by the boys of the neighbourhood because the old gentleman who lived there was their friend, and there was always a welcome for them; in fact, he spent a considerable amount of his time answering the door.

"Please, Mr. Pope, have you got a bicycle pump?"

"I say, Mr. Pope, have you got a rabbit hutch, because I know someone who has a rabbit?"

"Mr. Pope, got a padlock?"

"Would you like to see what I've got in my pocket, Mr. Pope?" And the old gentleman stooped down with the greatest interest, to be introduced to two white mice.

He kept a very well-stocked junk shed, and could nearly always manage to find what his visitors wanted; at least, he was never too busy to try. He also had in his garden, clock golf and bumble puppy which were in great demand, and sometimes boys just wanted to come in and have a read.

He was a very accessible old man. "Don't get big and pompous so that people won't come to you," he once wrote. "It is very easy for speakers, if they are not watchful, to become important and big. We need to pray against it, lest people be put off, and are afraid to approach us. Be accessible. The Lord was always so. The children ran to Him and flocked about Him."

He was well known in the local Scout Troop, where all had joined Scripture Union, and he had enrolled about five members on a nearby housing estate. On Sunday and Wednesday nights he had a boys' meeting, and a number were truly converted. He still occasionally accepted invitations to speak outside, and one of his greatest joys was a meeting for twenty-five Scouts in the cows' milking shed. The boys sat on groundsheets or in the feeding trough, and some sat on the partitions between the stalls. He held their attention, as ever.

It seemed a lot for a man of eighty-five, who had had a stroke, to be doing, and sometimes people remonstrated with him.

"But I *love* the work," he replied in self-defence. "I do feel tired, but the thought of another children's meeting refreshes me. When I speak, my voice gets strong. I can't do much, but I can carry on the S.U. work, and there are always the letters . . . and in the holidays, Jack will come."

But during school terms he lived alone, with what help he could muster. "I have secured a capable Christian housekeeper," he wrote "and another to come in on No. 1's half-days, and a third to scrub the floor twice a week, so the house is stiff with servants! I only want a butler, a chauffeur, a gardener, and a page-boy to complete the establishment."

He lived frugally and simply as he had always had to do, and there were no luxuries in the home. The great blank left by his wife's death probably never grew any less, but he would tell you that he had so much for which to praise God.

Perhaps his greatest cause for joy and praise were the trunks of children's letters, all carefully classified—the record of his life's work. Some of these letters dated back fifty years, and sometimes he browsed happily among them. "As I read all these records of God's goodness," he said, "I have been broken down with the wonder of it all. And when my thoughts go on to all the boys and girls who did not write to the evangelist, I am lost in wonder, love and praise. Some things stand out particularly as I read these letters.

> Conviction of sin.
> Reception of the Saviour.
> Resultant joy and victory.
> Answers to prayer expected and received.
> Desire for the salvation of others.
> The value of suitable literature and pictorial illustration."

Life had moulded him, for behind the busy-ness and joy of his campaigns he had had his private cares, temptations, and, at times, deep sorrows too intimate to write of. His only son's car accident in 1932, resulting in the amputation of his right arm, must have been a sore grief to both parents, especially in view of the boy's unusual musical ability. Some give hints of checks, disappointments, oppositions in his career which need never have been, but one never hears of these from Mr. Pope. As he grew older, he learned that there are no second causes, but took all, with thanksgiving, straight from the hand of his Father.

"Life is simply glorious, if not gloriously simple," he wrote to a friend.

But his wife's frequent ill-health, the clashing loyalties of his home ties and his work often tried him sorely, for his was a nature of extremes, and he could be as depressed as he could be exuberant; and he wrote freely of these times of testing to his closest friends.

"The last four months have been a time of great testing and great stress of work. What I expected has happened and my wife has had a breakdown. I had to come home in the middle of my mission, but when I got someone to live in I went back and finished it. What gives me concern is, ought I to give up my work for my wife's sake? I see no way to mend matters whichever way I look, and oh, how we have prayed about it! I am very, very tired, not so much physically as otherwise, and it is difficult sometimes to carry on. Does this sound like lack of faith? I hope it isn't, because I'm carrying on, and it is only His strength which enables me. His grace *is* sufficient."

"It is many months since I took a mission now. My heart longs to be at the work, but it seems as though the way is hedged up at present ... oh, how the devil assails my poor faith these days and says, 'Where is thy God?' Pray on for your poor weak brother, and I shall yet praise Him. But the praising time seems so long coming."

And then on April 30th, 1959, he wrote to Alwyn Harland:

"This morning at 4 a.m. the Lord called my dear one away; she passed gently into His arms. I am sore stricken, but rejoicing for her. Pray for me."

The nurse who attended her during her last illness was deeply impressed by the peace of that Home-going, and she herself found Christ. The special text they had shared through the years was engraved on her tombstone, "Jesus Himself drew near and went with them"; and he was comforted, as usual, by one of his little children.

"Aren't you frightened to walk through that churchyard all by yourself?" asked someone of a very small girl.

"Oh, no," replied the child smiling, "my home is just on the other side."

In 1960 he had retired officially from the Scripture Union staff at the age of eighty. A reception was held at Church House, Westminster, on November 14th. A large audience gathered, many of whom he had led to Christ through his ministry. Mr. W. G. Norris, former Chairman of the Scripture Union Council, led in a prayer of thanksgiving, and the then Chairman, Mr. Derek Warren, introduced four speakers, each of whom referred briefly to some aspect of Mr. Pope's life and work. Mr R. S. French, leader of Beaconsfield Crusader Class, spoke of a memorable mission in Cambridge when he, and a number of others well known in the Christian world, had discovered just what an illustrated talk was, and how effectively it could turn the whole course of a young man's life. Mr. Alwyn Harland, leader of Ballyholme C.S.S.M., and for many years a co-worker with Mr. Pope at seaside missions, reminded those present of the indefatigable energy and enthusiasm with which Mr. Pope did his work as leader. Dr. J. M. Laird, General Secretary of the Scripture Union, paid tribute to Mr. Pope as a colleague and member of the Mission staff. An acrostic on the word Pope provided him with four points he wanted to emphasize:

His adherence to	Principle;
His ready	Obedience to authority;
His	Perseverance for fifty-four years;
His steadfast concentration on	Evangelism.

Finally, Mr. E. P. Olney, then a member of the Scripture Union Council and R. H. P.'s lifelong friend, drew back the veil on some of the very early days of R. H. P.'s service, and their joint work among the telegraph boys of South London. Mrs. Warren then presented the Council's gift to Mr. Pope—a tape-recorder bearing a silver plate on which was inscribed a testimonial. Mrs. Warren recalled how she herself had been led to Christ through Mr. Pope.

Much of Mr. Pope's reply has been used in this biography, but the end of it is quoted verbatim—a wonderful retrospect of the struggles and conflicts through which he had passed, and his hope and confidence for the future.

"Do you think that it is an easy thing for a man to become a soul-winner in the service of the Lord? Do you think that somehow or other when a man gets older and has had experience that it gets simpler and easier as he gets older? It doesn't. 'Mr. Pope, you don't get great temptations and inward struggles!' Don't I? If you who are not on whole-time work for your Lord knew sometimes what those who are were feeling inside, you would be on your knees praying for us. The devilish devices that the Evil One brings to drag us away, to weaken our defences, until presently he is able to come in suddenly! And who of older Christians does not know that sometimes even some beloved Christian has fallen by the way? 'Let him that thinketh he standeth take heed lest he fall.' Oh, the devilish devices the Evil One brings—and not by making a great assault all at once on some particular part of the citadel and letting us know when he is coming. It is the steady whittling away, whittling away; a little bit of our Bible study gone, a little bit of our prayer-time gone, a lapse in carefulness—until the wall begins to crumble, and when he sees that there is going to be a nice weak spot, in he comes more suddenly than ever we would have imagined he would. Haven't some of us here tonight been pretty near the edge of the precipice in our own experience? If you knew this man as I know him, I almost think you would say, 'I am not going to listen to him.' If you knew this man as God knows him—oh, the struggles, oh, the inward fighting, oh, the earnest supplication to God for grace and strength!

"And then if sometime the Devil does get in, and we are not only on the edge of the precipice, but we are over the edge, he comes sneeringly to us and says, pointing to some thought or word or act which has escaped us in our hurry, 'Now go and preach!' You say, 'Sir, that kind of thing doesn't come in in the life of a man who wants to be up in the top storey of work for God.' Oh, that is just where it does. If Satan sees there is someone who is going to be a damage to his kingdom, if he sees there is somebody who is going to bowl him out, he will be careful to start the bowling first and bowl that one out, and then he'll say, 'Now go and preach!'

"And then we have to get down on our knees and get back. You say, 'Will the Lord have me?' Yes! Yes! Listen:

> "Unless the Lord had been my stay,
> With trembling joy my soul will say

—after I have sinned; and then,

> "Dismiss me not Thy service, Lord,
> But train me for Thy will;
> For even I, in fields so broad,
> Some duties may fulfil;
> And I will ask for no reward
> Except to serve Thee still."

The Joy of Arrival

* * * * *

*On June 4th, 1967, R. H. P.'s old friend Ted Olney died peacefully at the age of eighty-six. But, as this book goes to press, R. H. P. himself, at eighty-seven, lingers on. For him, the joy of arrival is postponed.

A visitor who called to see him in his hospital ward found him longing for release from frailty and at times mental distress. "Now I can't preach—please ask God to help me to say the right word."

His mind was dwelling on William Cowper's hymn "God moves in a mysterious way" and he was able to quote it in full. He lingered over the line: "The bud may have a bitter taste." He was obviously troubled as to why God had not taken him, and as to why he had to end his days in hospital and not in his own home. His visitor tried gently to comfort him: "But this is God's provision for you." "Yes", he said, "thank you for pulling me up." It was as if he was saying, "Thank you for your loving reminder, thank you for encouraging me to fight better and to accept what God allows. Thank you for nerving me to fight self-pity, thank you for being so faithful with me in my moment of weakness, thank you for reminding me that 'God is His own interpreter and He will make it plain'."

How often R. H. P. had done just this for other people. Lovingly, wisely, humorously, understandingly, he had pulled us up at moments when we certainly needed a steadying word. Now someone had done it for him. And in his humility and desire to be at all times the best for God, and with his unfailing courtesy, his reaction, typical of a lifetime of self-discipline, was just this: "Thank you for pulling me up."

When, in the *Pilgrim's Progress*, Christian and his friend, Hopeful, came to the last River, Christian began to sink in the water, and crying out to his good friend Hopeful, he said, "I Sink in deep Waters; the Billows go over my head, all his Waves go over me". Then said the other, "Be of good cheer my Brother, I feel the bottom, and it is good . . ." "Here (Christian) in great measure lost his senses, so that he could neither remember, nor orderly talk of any of these sweet refreshments that he had met with in the way of his Pilgrimage. . . . Hopeful therefore had much

---

* This and the next four paragraphs were written by Dr. John M. Laird, in the absence of the author in North Africa.

ado to keep his Brother's head above water; yea, sometimes he would be quite gone down . . ." till, at last, he was able to hold on to the promise: "When thou passest through the Waters, I will be with thee; and through the Rivers, they shall not overflow thee. Then they both took courage, and the Enemy was after that as still as a stone, until they were gone over."

* * * * *

Long ago, R. H. P. had written this about his Saviour:

"He will come in, and He will stay to supper. Which meal is supper? Quite right, the last. It is the morning of your day now, and as you open the door to Him the bright morning sun streams into your heart. And He has said He will stay to supper—the very end of the day—after supper we shall go to bed, 'lulled to sleep by Jesus', the Bible calls it, and when we wake up it will be morning. The day is far spent for some of us older folk, but cheer up, it's quite all right! He is staying to supper."

BV   St. John
3785
.P6   R. Hudson Pope
S2